SINGLE, SAVED,

AND

HAVING

SEX

TY ADAMS

Single, Saved, And Having Sex

© Copyright 2002, 2006 Ty Adams
3rd Edition

**Heaven Enterprises
20318 Grand River Detroit, MI 48219**
www.TyAdamsTV.com

Printed in the United States of America

ALL RIGHTS RESERVED

This book is protected under the copyright laws of the United States of America. No portion of this book may be reproduced in any form or by any means--electronic, mechanical, photocopying, recording or otherwise--without the written permission of the publisher. Permission granted upon request. Unless otherwise noted, Scripture quotations are from the King James Version of the Bible.

Unless otherwise marked, Scripture quotations are from The Holy Bible, New King James Version copyright © 1979, 1980, 1982 by Thomas Nelson, Inc.

Scripture noted AMP are taken from the Amplified New Testament copyright © 1958, 1987 by The Lockman Foundation. Used by permission.

Scripture noted MSG are taken from THE MESSAGE. Copyright © by Eugene H. Peterson, 1993, 1994, 1995, 1996. Used by permission of NavPress Publishing Group.

Scripture quotation marked (NTL) are taken from the Holy Bible, New Living Translation. Copyright © 1996. Used by permission of Tyndale Home Publishers, Inc., Wheaton, Illinois 60819. All rights reserved.

FOREWORD

One of the greatest fallouts of this era was the disregard for the sanctity of sexual commitment and the honoring of marriage and the acceptable confines for such behavior. The result is a generation of sex-crazed individuals with little regard for discipline, respect and commitment. This culture has invaded the Christian church, and believers find themselves struggling with sexual pressure and habits that were once a part of their lives before they came to the church. This creates a great dilemma for the church and a challenge for leaders to address this issue just as the Apostle Paul had in his day.
I realized there are millions of people who need to receive counsel and advice about this serious and personal aspect of life. Unfortunately, most of the advice is based upon cheap psychology and paperback reports of experiences not founded upon truth.

It is my strong conviction and logical conclusion that any discussion or exploration of our personal lifestyles must be approached from a biblical perspective. In *Single, Saved, and Having Sex,* Ty Adams presents a no compromising lifestyle that takes you through the process of renewing your mind through the knowledge of God's Word. She clearly reveals that there should be NO compromising as she introduces the Holy Spirit as the Ultimate Guide in our lives.

Ty has taken the bull by the horns and delivers a direct, candid and much-needed approach in this untapped subject of sexual struggle among singles, both young and old. Ty's frank and gripping approach provides you with the tools necessary to deal with the temptations and pressures around you, to overcome with dignity. This book also demands that you take responsibility for your own life and dedicate yourself to the standards set out by the Word of God. Ty leaps over complicated theological theory and brings us face-to-face with the realities of temptation, but also gives answers to singles who still need to know and understand the holiness and purity of the gift of sex created by God and the context within which it is to be enjoyed.

As you embrace Ty's words of wisdom, you will feel compelled to examine your life personally with the anticipation of making the necessary adjustments to produce a life-changing transformation. When you finish reading Single, Saved, and Having Sex, you will experience Ty's passion for others to never settle for anything less than God's best for their lives. You cannot remain the same after you have embraced what the Lord delivers through her in this powerful, newly expanded book.

Dr. Myles Munroe
Bestselling author, *In Pursuit of Purpose*
Founder and President of Bahamas Faith Ministries
CEO of International Third World Development

CONTENTS

PART ONE: OUR QUEST FOR INTIMACY

Chapter One: Single, Saved, and Having Sex   6
Chapter Two: Reliving The Past   22
Chapter Three: Committing Spiritual Adultery   44

PART TWO: FINDING WHO WE ARE IN CHRIST

Chapter Four: Breaking Free From The Identity Crisis   62
Chapter Five: Reclaiming Your Body   75
Chapter Six: Reclaiming Your Mind   86

PART THREE: THE PATH TO WHOLENESS

Chapter Seven: Healing Your Heart   110
Chapter Eight: Finding Mr. Right   126
Chapter Nine: The Lover of Your Soul   153

Chapter One: Single, Saved and Having Sex

"You're addicted to thrills? What an empty life! The pursuit of pleasure is never satisfied."
Proverbs 21:17 Message

The sexual revolution of the 1960's has cast us into an age of low moral values and promiscuity. If you are a single woman or man, there is pressure to become a sexual being from society, television, music, advertising and your peers.

But now, more than ever, people of all ages are feeling less emotionally attached, more vacant and empty-even if their beds are filled with lovers and their social lives sizzle. And most of these people call themselves Christians. In fact, seventy percent of all unmarried Christians are saved and having sex.

The quest for intimacy and fulfillment is at an all-time high. Over the last year, just about every magazine on the newsstands featured articles on sex and relationships. With titles like, "When should you give *it* up?" "How do I please my man sexually?" and "How do I heal from a broken relationship?" We are constantly bombarded with one message: sex is all that matters and it had better be good.

Single dating shows have become popular and among the highest rated programs on TV. These shows are comprised of single men and women who have the opportunity of dating 20 people in one night or competing for a relationship with a rich man, one whom they barely get to know.

E-mail is full of pop-ups inviting you to go to a dating site and online dating services and chat rooms are swamped with people searching for a physical relationship or a way to hook up with a member of the opposite sex as quickly and painlessly as possible. Yet a large percentage of single people who struggle with relationships and are having sex either believe in or love God, this same God who only approves of sex if you are married. Does this prove that you, a single person, can believe in or love God the way He requires us to love Him and still have sex?

God created and designed you to have wholeness in every area of your life. We have physical, emotional, social, mental and spiritual needs that need to be fulfilled. When we have a need for intimacy, we quickly respond physically. That's because we live in a microwave, fast-food mentality age; we want quick, instant gratification. We want it our way, right away; we want it fast and it better be satisfying.

We've tried to acquire intimacy in an instant—in a 6-second orgasm, a temporary relief that takes you back down to where you were before you took off your clothes. But once the morning after syndrome sets in, you wake up and find out that you didn't get what you were seeking. Then, even though you realize that your needs weren't met, you continue your quest for fulfillment through physical mean, while your spiritual and mental departments hang in limbo.

Now, ever-increasing failed relationships and sexual partnerships become the norm. You move on to another relationship, they don't work out, you move on to another bed partner. Like an addiction, you are consumed with achieving another climax. This is known as "the thrill is gone" syndrome—when the immediate gratification thrills and pleasures of sex leave, you move right on to the next bed. Like me, some of you, after a few rock-bottom relationships, begin to work on the other departments. You start praying, may even start going to church, but you continue to get intimacy physically. You give some of yourself over to God, but you find yourself living a double life. This is commonly known as "your body's here with me, but your mind is on the other side of town."

You will soon realize that trying to meet the quest for intimacy by physical means will begin to add up. Or have you not weighed and counted up the cost? For singles, sex is never free. What price would you put on a damaged or wounded heart? How much does AIDS or HIV cost? How about a life with no peace, what kind of price tag would you put on that? How much does it cost to kill a baby? Or what's the price on a bankrupt spirit? Oh, here's one, how much does it cost to go to hell?

The question again is, is it possible to believe in or love God and still have sex? I don't know if that's really the question because I can guess that many of you don't love sex to the point that you would be willing to pay the high cost for it. Especially the cost of being separated eternally from the God you love. Yet, you somehow continue to pray, go to church, proclaim the name of Jesus—while you engage in sexual activities. I know exactly what that's like to love God but find it hard to please Him because of wild, rampant sexual desires that need to be fulfilled. I know what it's like to want to live right but at the same time wanting to be held.

Many of you believe that your sexual exploits will be excused by such a loving and understanding God. Some of you, on the other hand, believe that eventually, you'll get things under control when you get the guts to leave the relationship or your sexual partner, to fully live for God. There are many of you who have left the church because your struggle with sex outweighed your capacity to live right for God and the other percentage of you are still going to church faithfully and cover up the fact that you are having sex. Either case, I want to share something with you that Dr. Mike Murdock often states: **"Struggle is proof that you have not yet been conquered."** My prayer is that those of you who find yourself in the struggle will finally obtain the answers that you need to overcome and walk away "Single, Saved, and NOT Having Sex."

But I know this isn't going to be easy. Why? Because everywhere we look, it's sex, sex, sex, sex, sex—get it as much as you can, when you can, with whomever you can. This is what's depicted throughout the nation in our TV, in the news, and the radio. Turn on the TV and a toothpaste commercial will have two people hugging and kissing. You can't look at a shampoo commercial without a sexual connotation in it. Now, what does washing your hair have to do with having sexual pleasure? Let's not talk about the movies and music. There is no in-between—"Maybe that's what they're talking about." There are no hidden messages; it's flat-out X-rated!

You have so many opinions and different beliefs about sex coming at you. You grow up trained to think and believe a certain way about sex. You're not a man unless you have a few women; you need to have all the flavors and if they don't satisfy you, "handle yourself." If you're a virgin, something has to be wrong." As for a woman, you need a man to complete you and you have to outdo the other women he's been with in bed in order to keep him. Sound familiar?

Here we are, living our entire lives with these man-made ideas of how sex should be—with whomever we want—then you get "saved." This is where a major problem lies. The spirit of a man is changed, but his mind isn't changed. This is one reason why high rates of single folks in the church have active sex lives. We come with this going-out-the-world backwards thinking, with the mindset of not changing the way we live our lives and not turning away from these beliefs that have been embedded in us; a new spirit, but the same mind. If that's not enough, we go back to the same resources for advice when it all falls apart.

Okay, let me give you a mental picture. I was driving a brown 1981 Cutlass, it was dented in the rear end and gaseous fumes were coming out of the tailpipe. I was sharp, looking good, but when I would get out the car, I would smell like a walking exhaust system. When it broke down, I would not take it to the shop and get it fixed. I would take the car, dent and all, to what we call "alley mechanics" (mechanics who fix cars in backyards or in front of their houses).

Now, picture a Mercedes Benz 700 Series, white, leather interior—no fumes. It needs to be serviced (notice I said serviced). Would you take it to an "alley mechanic"? Oh, no! You would take it to the dealer, the manufacturer. That's the same thing with you; you are no longer a broke down, barely making-it '81 Cutlass with poisonous fumes. You are in a new class, a new series of your life and you can't go and get quick fixes from unskilled folks giving you experimental advice. You go to the Manufacturer.

God, your Manufacturer, created you and He created sex. Why would you go to the alley sex mechanic for help and ask about either of the two? Since God created sex and He created you, He knows your hang-ups, your shortcomings, faults, desires, why you respond and act a certain way, and He has the solution should you malfunction. If you are having issues or struggling with something that He created, by all means, He should be the one that you go to for help. Remember this: **Sexual sin: of or involving sex, the two sexes, or the sexual organs in a willful violation of a religious or moral principle; sexually unrestrained by morality; any wrong or evil act involving sex, the two sexes, or the sexual organs.**

There are quite a few of you who believe that sexual intercourse is only when a man enters into a woman's vagina. Sexual intercourse is defined as an intimate physical relationship, especially between a man and a woman, involving the **use** of the sexual organs. This means that even if a man does not enter a woman but has physical contact with the woman with any use of the sexual organs, that is having sexual intercourse; it's the course or path of entering into sex.

Let me translate that for you: this also means that foreplay (the acts that happen before a man enters into a woman) is considered sexual intercourse/the course or path of entering into sex. Examples of foreplay include heavy petting, fondling, and yes, even tongue kissing. This even includes masturbation—the stimulation of one's own or another's genitals/self sex. Masturbation is a downward spiral effect because it is the act of living out your past on yourself. You are responding to twisted sexual perversions that have developed in your mind that cause you to believe that gratification by any means will fulfill a desire or need. Masturbation breeds confusion and leaves you in a greater degree of discontentment and emptiness.

Pornography is considered sexual immorality or fornication, which comes from the Greek word "porneia," which is defined as illicit sexual activity. Pornography is any literature, art, magazines, movies, music, or photography of erotic or sexual acts intended to excite prurient feelings (tending to have lustful thoughts). I needed to define that for some of you who think you do not engage in pornography because you don't have videos or X-rated magazines with erotic or sexual acts in them. Illicit, erotic, X-rated or vulgar movies or music are forms of pornography. You know, the kind of music that talks about your body parts and what he/she is going to do with those body parts, yeah, that's pornographic music.

Oh, did I fail to mention oral and anal sex? Now, the fact that some of you think that oral or anal sex is not sex kinda confuses me. Sex in the word alone gives you a big clue and indicates that it is sex. If you are using the sexual organs, that is considered sexual intercourse. So putting your mouth on **any** sexual organ is sexual sin. The anus was placed on your body to defecate or remove waste, not to put waste in it. Waste is anything barren, unproductive, unfruitful, devoid (not to use), or uninhabited (not to dwell in). To engage in anal sex is a **wasteful** act, you are not to dwell there. Listen, single man or woman, if you have either oral or anal sex, you are considered a sodomite, which comes from the word sodomy. **Sodomy is defined as the**

unnatural, especially anal or oral, use of copulation/sexual intercourse.

"Then the Lord rained on Sodom and on Gomorrah brimstone and fire from the Lord out of the heavens. He overthrew, destroyed, and ended those cities, and all the valley and all the inhabitants of the cities, and what grew on the ground." Genesis 19:24, 25 Amplified

God destroyed the entire city of Sodom and Gomorrah because of its sinful, sexual perversion. I can see some of your faces now, "Oh, blessed Jesus, I can't believe she put this in this book, I can't believe she went there. She is talking so openly about it." That's the problem now, we've been sugarcoating this for far too long; as quiet as it's kept, some of you talk about it and actually do these things behind closed doors and cover it up and don't talk about it. Talking about covering up, there are a lot of undercover Christians literally under the covers and the only way a lot of you are going to be delivered and set free is to go under the covers where you are and grab you out. So, let's uncover.

Now, this would not be complete if we didn't talk about homosexuality, which we'll get in-depth with later. It is defined as exhibiting sexual desires toward a person of one's own sex. I had to clarify and define some things because we look at sin in levels and degrees as if one carries more weight than the other. "I don't watch pornography," but you listen to it on your favorite radio station. "I don't sleep around, I'm celibate," but you take care of yourself by masturbating. You would even have the audacity to turn your nose up at someone that comes to your church and appears to be a homosexual, but you're headed right for the hotel with someone you are not married to before the pastor can even give the benediction.

Surprisingly, I've had some people tell me, both men and women, that they are not in sexual sin because whenever they get with their bed partners, they may not actually penetrate a woman but they'll have oral sex with one another. Whichever way you put it, sexual penetration, masturbation, foreplay, tongue kissing, homosexuality, oral sex, anal sex, and pornography are all considered sexual intercourse; they are all sexual sins and are considered **fornication. Fornication is voluntary sexual intercourse between two unmarried persons or two persons not married to each other.**

> *"For this is the will of God, even your sanctification, that ye should abstain from fornication." I Thessalonians 4:3*

Picture a big, fat, pink pig running around in a muddy pigsty eating everything you throw at it. You get close to the pigsty and you notice that this pig has red lipstick on, high-heeled shoes, and a ring in its nose. Do you now look at the pig and say, "You are so cute"? No, you don't. The filth she's running in and her habit of eating everything that's foul, overpowers the lipstick and the gold ring. She's not cute at all, she's a filthy pig. Even Scripture tells us:

> *"As a ring of gold in a swine's snout, So is a lovely woman who lacks discretion." Proverbs 11:22*[2]

> *"Like a gold ring in a pig's snout is a beautiful face on an empty head." (The Message)*

When King Solomon spoke of this to the women in his day, about their indiscreet lifestyle, he had to compare it to what they believed was the filthiest thing ever. At that time, a swine was considered the filthiest animal. You wouldn't be caught dead eating a pork chop or a slice of bacon. Jewelry and gold nose rings were the hippest thing happening. When you saw a nose ring on a woman, it was absolutely beautiful! King Solomon was basically saying to the women, "You can't dress up ugly. You can't dress up in mess and filth."

He compared a foul pig with a gold ring in its nose to a drop-dead gorgeous woman who was not tactful, who lacked judgment and the ability to make quality decisions in her life. You are a dressed-up wild, foul pig. Just as a gold ring couldn't cover up a filthy pig, neither could a woman's pretty face and shapely body cover up nor cancel out the fact that she lacks moral discretion. A pretty face without discretion is useless and has no worth or value. Men, take notes. The last thing you want or need is a woman who lacks the ability to exercise good judgment or tact. The Word of Go d tell us "He that finds a wife, finds a good thing." Proverbs 18:22 Ladies, you are not considered "a good thing" if you do not possess or exercise good judgment.

> Good: morally excellent, proper, fit, well behaved, honorable or worthy, sound or valid, not spoiled or tainted, competent, and morally righteous.

You can't be a good thing if you lack good judgment . . . and you can't possess good judgment without the "goods," without being tainted. You must also be morally excellent. The only way that you possess the "goods" is through goodness, as indicated in the Message Translation in Psalms 119, V. 68.

> *"You are good, and the source of good; train me in your goodness."*

Now that you have goodness, you need to understand that you already possess the goods. You have not yet tapped into them. It means nothing to possess the "goods" if you don't exercise or walk in what you have. Now, in order to become what you already are or maintain good judgment in your every day life or in your practical affairs, you have to give God the consent in your affairs.

So, what are your practical affairs? What do you spend your time doing on a daily basis? Who are your friends? What does your "play" time consist of? What do you spend your weekend doing? What do you do when you get home from work? What you decide to do on a daily basis is who you are. You are made up of the sum total of the choices and decisions you make everyday. Whenever you have fallen short of God's Will, you can trace it back to what you were doing before it happened. There's no "oops" about it. "Oops, I don't know how I got here in this bed with my pants off. Oops, there goes my shirt!" Stuff doesn't "just happen." **There's a set-up before the mess up.**

The habits you've created were produced out of practice. A habit does not form without practice. The word "practical" derives from the word "practice" (a repeated or habitual performance). So, let's call them practiced affairs. Again, what are you repeatedly doing on a day-to-day basis? Okay, I know you're repeatedly having sex, but what are you doing to get there? There are some things that are happening before you engage in or practice sexual acts. We talked about it in the previous chapter, but let's look at it some more from the Word, Mark chapter 7, V18-19, and 20-23:

> *"Jesus said, 'Are you willfully stupid? Don't you see that what you swallow can't contaminate you? It doesn't enter your heart but your stomach, work its way through the intestines, and is finally flushed.' . . . He went on: 'It's what comes out of a person that pollutes: obscenities, lusts, adulteries . . . all these are vomit from the heart. There is the source of your pollution.'"*
>
> *"What comes out of the mouth gets its start in the heart. It's from the heart that we vomit fornication." Matthew 15:16 (Message)*

Evil thoughts and lewdness (excessive sexual indulgence) were also included as a defilement of the heart. So, how do sexual immorality, fornication, evil thoughts and lewdness get into the heart? I'm glad you asked. The Bible says in Matthew chapter 6 and 22 that "Your eyes are windows into your body . . ." The mouth, the ears, and the eyes are the gates to your heart. Sexual immorality either came through the gates of your eyes, ears, or your mouth, through the door of your heart. I worked in the media and marketing/advertising industry for several years. On an average day, it is said that you will take in between 3,000 to 5,000 impressions. An impression is a strong effect produced on the intellect, feelings, or conscience (usually produced by pressure) so as to leave a mark.

So, what's impressing you? Daily, you take in about 3,000 to 5,000 impressions through TV, music, newspaper, radio or pass by billboards, etc., that will leave a mark on your intellect (your understanding), feelings (your emotions, sensations), and your conscience (the sense of what is right or wrong in one's conduct). Once it gets into you, it goes to the heart, leaves a mark and eventually, you'll act it out, then it'll become your practiced affairs. Now, I know your favorite TV program is lawful, but is it helpful? What about the movies you go out on the weekend to see? Is it helpful or does it incite sexual immorality?

> *"Everything is permissible (allowable and lawful) for me but not all things are helpful (good for me to do, expedient and profitable when considered with other things). Everything is lawful for me, but I will not become the slave of anything or be brought under its power." I Corinthians 6:12 Amplified*

Okay, some of you make light of your "pass-by time" and think that it will not affect you. "The movies and the music I listen to do not affect my walk with Christ." That's the farthest from the truth. Why do you think companies spend millions of dollars on advertising? They know that the impressions will leave a mark on you and incite you to action, to impress you to "obey your thirst" or "just do it." These impressions work through your faculties or your senses: what you see, what you hear, taste, feel and touch. **If I can get to your mind, it's nothing for me to get your body to respond.**

Everything around you is either a ministry or a seed planter. The word administration derives from the word administer or ministry. It's planting a seed whether you realize it or not, and that seed is planted in your heart through the gates of your ears, eyes or your mouth. Your television is planting a seed; it tells a vision (tel-e-vision) by the broadcasting of images.

Images are how your thought patterns are created. Your radio is a powerful influence or impression. Music is very influential and it incites or impacts the way you think and act. Your Bible holds the hugest music department in it: Psalms. It's the largest book in the Bible and it was placed right in the center . . . and guess who created music?

God knew the very essence of music would be powerful, so powerful that it has defeated armies in battle, so powerful that it takes you into the presence of God. Now, satan, the mishap that he is, went and distorted music. He knew how powerful music was, since he was the minister of music with speakers in his chest that would shatter your eardrums. He distorted it in such a way that party-goers will throw their hands up to it. Does "wave your hands in the air and wave 'em like you just don't care," ring a bell? Lifting up your hand in worship was instituted by the Almighty God, and the influence of music is being used in an evil, ungodly manner. That perpetrating devil is a fabricator and he uses music to draw you to sexual immorality.

Now, I'm not saying that all music is bad, but there's so much pornographic music on the radio that it's difficult to sift through it to even get to the good music. Okay, the music that encourages you to have sex in the words of "drop it like it's hot or back that thang up," yeah, that kind of music. "You can take your clothes off here, we can do it anywhere, I don't care." Music that's illicit and vulgar, that describes sexual acts in a wicked manner . . . and some of you just bop your head to it. Oh, because you like the beat. Haven't I heard that quite a bit, while you bop all the way to the hotel?

It's supposed to have a good beat. Pornographic music will arouse you and it will influence and persuade your emotions. How many times have you listened to that song that talked about him knowing where your "spot" is? That's how that strange man got to your heart in the first place. It made you think about him and before you knew it, you picked up the phone and called him. Do you actually think that you can listen to that type of music that describes a sex scene and not be moved by it? Before you put the hotel key in the doorknob, it started out as a thought. When you speak and sing the lyrics, it goes into your subconscious mind and stores itself there. The thought was planted by the song, you danced to it, and then you acted on it.

If music wasn't such an influence, it wouldn't have the stronghold it has on some of you and you'd just turn the radio off, but you'd rather make excuses and try to convince someone that it's not so bad. I know, it was hard for me to let it go because I excused myself in the name of "it's not all that bad." I loved music. I did, and I still do. I love music but I asked myself, "How bad is your want to?" I admittedly kept telling God, "I want to be right, I want to stop fornicating. I want to so bad . . ." In the same breath, I would turn on music that enticed me to sin. So, how bad is your "want to"?

I remember one time I was fasting and I said that I would not listen to music. That was extremely hard! It was only the Holy Spirit that kept me from turning the radio on in the car for 30 straight days. After the fast, I went back to my daily regimen and turned the radio back on when I jumped in the car. "Old school" music was on and I was in the car jammin'! For the first couple of songs, the music was cool. By the time the third song came on, I was singing out of my mouth, "Have sex with me until it kills me." That's what the song actually said. I hurried to turn the radio off! Sex is never so good that I'd for it. I had entered into a marriage with sexual sin "'til death do us part." I was at the point where I was willing to divorce it at all costs.

The Lord revealed to me, right there, that if I wanted to maintain my deliverance, I would have to let it go. No, not let music go. I could no longer listen to music that He didn't create. There is power in your tongue and every time you sing and speak words out of your mouth, they manifest themselves in your life. You sing your way right into sexual sin. My eyes were so blind that I didn't even realize that there was gospel music that was not only good for my soul, but also good to my ears. What I mean by that is there's some really good gospel music to listen to. I was shocked because I was still able to jam!

I remember going to the movies one night with my friends for a "girls' night out." Now, let me tell you, we had just finished a powerful Friday night of prayer and watching Bishop T. D. Jakes' videos, and shouting through the apartment. It was about ten o'clock and they suggested that we go to the movies. I wasn't going to go and my friend said, "Come on and go. The last movie you went to see was *Shaft;* the first one!" She was sort of right, so we ran over to the theater, grabbed some popcorn and the moment we sat down, naked butts splashed all across the screen. I thought, "Okay, maybe that was just the first part of it. The movie will calm down now and it'll get pass this part."

It got worse! You remember back in the day when they didn't show a man's genitals? This movie did, and it seemed as if the screen held it in that area for a good, long two minutes. I covered up my eyes like a 'lil girl and screamed, "Oh, my God!" All my friends were laughing. "I don't know why ya'll laughing. I haven't seen one of 'those' since 1960. Let's go!"

I was serious, too. There I was, fresh out of sexual sin, and looking at pornography. That's exactly what it was: porn wrapped up as a movie. There's no way you can be a "kept" man or woman—kept from sexual sin—watching sexually explicit movies. Moreover, some of the sitcoms that are on TV are just trashy as ever. Anything that causes you to slip, stumble or flat-out fall into sin, GET RID OF IT!

> *"If your hand or foot gets in the way of God, chop it off and throw it away. You're better off maimed or lame and alive than the proud owners of two hands and two feet, godless in a furnace of eternal fire. And if your eye distracts you from God, pull it out and throw it away. You're better off one-eyed and alive than exercising your twenty-twenty vision from inside the fire of hell."*
> Matthew 18:18 (Message)

Of course, you can't literally chop your hand off or cut your eye out, but the Word is saying that if what your eye is watching distracts you from God, then pull it out and throw it away. Pull your eye from watching it and throw away whatever is getting in the way of you and God, for it is better to let that ungodly music or those movies go than to burn in hell for it. But what happens when you pull out your eye and yet you are still struggling with sexual sin? Let's look at a letter I received from a woman who found out about my book during one of my TV appearances, who dealt with this very issue.

"I am 33 years old and still a virgin and plan on staying that way 'til marriage. Some years ago I got hooked on pornography by watching an adult rated TV program. After battling with it for a long while, I praise God because I got a hold of your book. I repented and got delivered—I even got rid of cable! Now, I watch mostly TBN, Daystar and family type programs. My problem is that every now and then those same old urges come back and I don't understand why. I try to be careful of what I put before my eyes and ears. Why do I still sometimes get sexual urges? Signed, Beverly."

I commend you greatly for taking a stance for purity and living holy before the Lord. Beverly you've made the necessary changes in your life and placed a guard over your eyes and ears and that also is to be commended. I know you're serious if you got rid of your cable! Often times the Lord will deliver His people but many Christians don't make the necessary changes to maintain deliverance but the Lord will certainly honor your commitment to holiness and you shall see the rewards thereof. I thank God that He has delivered you from pornography and from the sexual snares of the enemy but I must tell you, Beverly, there's one thing you'll never be delivered from. It's a ten-lettered word called: TEMPTATION!

> There is nothing wrong with you. You are perfectly fine. Having a sexual urge is perfectly normal. In fact, you're going to need it once you get married! Until then, it's what you do with that urge will determine the

consequences or rewards in your life. If you look in Luke 4 when satan came to tempt Jesus, you'll find that after the temptation ended, it says in verse 13 that satan departed for a season. Let's look at this in the Amplified Bible.

"And when the devil had ended every [the complete cycle of] temptation, he [temporarily] left him [that is, stood off from Him] until another more opportune and favorable time."

Just like Beverly, me and even you, we'll never be delivered from temptation. Movies and music are just a few of the temptations facing you. As long as you are on this earth, from time to time you'll meet temptation head on. If you are not staring it in the face now, don't let your guard down, satan only left you for the time being. So, if its always going to constantly be in your face, I guess we had better learn how to deal with the temptation so that we won't continue to fall prey to its never ending cycle. Let's stay ahead of him and discover when is satan's favorable time and how to not yield and succumb to the temptation when it comes. Read on.

Chapter Two: Reliving The Past

> "No, dear brothers and sisters, I am still not all I should be, but I am focusing all my energies on this one thing: Forgetting the past and looking forward to what lies ahead."
> Philippians 3:13 NLT

Temptation is all around us and satan is constantly after us trying to chain us to our past, that troubled life that we lived before we came to Jesus. Ex-boyfriends, Mike, Robert, Tony, David…I could go on and I'm sure you could, too. Certainly there is no shortage of ex's in my past. As I look back, I can remember some 'fun' times but without a doubt the painful experiences these relationships left me with overshadows the temporary oohs and aahhs. I have to ask myself if the spin on the amusement ride was worth the high-priced lessons I had to pay for them. I had a long trail of men waiting in line to get on my roller coaster.

You know what it's like, waiting in a long line at the park to twirl and scream for 3 minutes, then get off with a dizzy, head spin, barely able to walk straight. Okay, maybe you've been saved all your life, but I was signing up more people for hell than satan was. I thought I was having some real fun but I was loving something that was killing me. I was a whore and didn't even know it! I was so blinded by satan that I overlooked my whorish lifestyle because I didn't walk the streets, my tricks came to my house or I went to theirs. I didn't label them "clients", but boyfriends". Like many of you, I was convinced that having him throw on a condom protected me. Yet why would I lay with anyone if he could ultimately kill me-either physically through disease or spiritually through hell. I was blinded by stupidity!

My 'way' of life was reality to me. It was virtually normal for me to open up the park everyday for folks to come in to play. After the ride was over, next.... When I realized a particular man in my life was causing me more pain than I could handle, the relationship was ended and I went on to the next one.

It's interesting, though, how I sometimes forgot the pain that was inflicted when an ex called to come and get a free re-*feel*. Okay, now some of you are acting like you don't know what I'm talking about. Alright, help me out, brother. You know how a guy can call a girl knowing he's not interested in a committed relationship but only wants to get his surface wet? It's almost like premeditated murder. His calculated, well-thought-out plan to seduce her back into the sheets is well rehearsed before he picks up the phone. Then, the mind games begin. He knows exactly what to say, how to rewind and then replay the memories you two created. He reminds you of the good times you had together, 'doesn't know how he ever let a good thing go', and because traces of him are still on the inside of you, he's standing in your bedroom getting free re-Feels before you know it. You would think after a while that intelligent people wouldn't continue to fall for the same trick, but all too often this same scenario is replayed in the lives of bible-carrying Christians. Let's look at an email that I received from a young lady in this same situation.

"I am a Christian woman, aged 29 and I'm in love with someone who is already involved with another lady. As I have known this, I decided to do away with him but he keeps telling me that he and this lady don't get along well and that I should hold on to him because he's going to make things become right between us. He says that he wants to end this relationship in a way that no one will be hurt. The problem I have with him is that he has told me about this other lady but this other lady doesn't know anything about me and he wants me not to expose anything between us. Please help/advise me on this matter. Is this man really genuine or is he just using me? Should I really wait for him to clear up things with this lady?" (See website for our Q & A)

Many of you don't readily welcome these pit-filled traps. Maybe you tell yourself you're not really going to go "all the way", you just want to be "held" but you succumb to the smooth jargon of his manipulation of mere words. It's interesting how one can think they are not really having sex because they are not going "all the way". Yet, even virgins can wake up in hell. There will be many virgin prostitutes spending eternity with satan, because even though they haven't gone all the way with sexual intercourse, they have performed sexual activities like oral sex and masturbation, either as the receiver or the giver.

Countless people lift up their hands on Sunday morning and then turn their hands on themselves on Monday. Masturbation is a stronghold and will have you held captive to your own will. Simply put, masturbation will master you. Perverted satan coerced you into molesting yourself and you become an accomplice in your own victimization. Those who are imprisoned by its grip find it extremely difficult to say no to its domineering lure. You become trapped in your mind and this thought stronghold tells you that the only way that you can escape the pain or longing in your life is to fondle yourself. Thus you become addicted to it. You are controlled by it and once you start, you have to keep doing it. The reverse happens though; because masturbation is satan's way of sex, it will turn on you after you use it. You start masturbating because you think that it will satisfy you but it ends up controlling you. You think your sexual desire will be fulfilled and that your loneliness will end, but you end up crying afterwards because you are consumed with shame and guilt and the space in your bed next to you is even colder.

Masturbation is lust. When you lay there and violate yourself. The thoughts you have to generate and develop during this sexual act are wicked and immoral. You manipulate your thoughts to develop sexual arousal and somehow the devil has made you believe that you are not having sex. Or you look at pornography to arouse yourself. Yet the Bible says in Matthew 5:28 (Amplified):

"But I say to you that everyone who so much as looks at a woman with evil desire for her has already committed adultery with her in his heart."

If you look at someone with evil desire, not touch, but look, you have already operated in sexual sin. The Message translation says "don't even think you've preserved your virtue simply by staying out of bed. Your heart can be corrupted by lust even quicker than your body. Those leering looks you think nobody notices-they also corrupt." The lust and wicked fantasies generated through masturbation corrupt you. If you think because no one else is not there in on this act with you, that you are not having sex, you are sadly mistaken. Cleary, masturbation is sex; it is self-sex. You are having sex with yourself and God never created self-sex. He created sex to be enjoyed by two people in covenant of marriage and if He didn't create masturbation then satan did. Understand this, when satan creates something, everything attached to it is wicked. You open a door and invite satan to inflict you with its immoral ruin. If you are masturbating and you are a woman, then you are having sex with a woman and you invite a lesbian spirit upon you. If you are masturbating and you are a man, then you are having sex with a man and you invite a homosexual spirit upon you. You molest yourself, you are assaulting yourself and it will hunt you.

I had a male Christian named Richard, 47 years old, who called my office for prayer after seeing me talk about this very thing on TBN's Praise the Lord. This man told me that he believed he was living celibate while he waited for the Lord to send him a wife. He had not had sexual intercourse for some time but was tempted by satan to start masturbating because his 'waiting season' was longer than he had hoped. He thought he should have been married by now. He told me he asked the Lord in frustration what was taking Him so long to send a wife. He said the Lord responded, "Why would I send you a wife when you are already having sex with yourself?" This grown man then began to weep like a baby as he painfully conveyed how lust had consumed his mind.

As the tears streamed his face, he said, "It was not by chance that I saw you on TV. I knew the Lord wanted to deliver me from masturbation because you were describing my life. When I first started, I thought it was harmless. I only did it when I got lonely but now I don't have any control and do it constantly; even when I don't want to do it. I tell myself that I'm not going to do it; I know that it's not of God, but I am overcome by my thoughts. I am tormented in my mind. In the beginning I would fantasize about me being with a woman, then that changed to several women. I've never been attracted to men, never, but the fantasies are with me having sex with men now. I hate this, I know this is not of God, and I want to be delivered, Lord, I'm sorry, please, help me…"

"For all that is in the world-the lust of the flesh [craving for sensual gratification] and the lust of the eyes [greedy longings of the mind] and the pride of life [assurance in one's own resources or in the stability of earthly things]-these do not come from the Father but are from the world [itself]." I John 2:16 (The Amplified)

Masturbation in its core root is evil and it does not come from God, but satan. You are fulfilling the lust of the flesh when you masturbate, consequently, reaping all that hell has to offer. When God created sex, He said, "I'm going to give my kids a gift that they will absolutely love. It's going to be like money, everybody's going to want it. But because of its power, you just can't use this gift just any ole' way. If truth be told, you can't allow its power and pleasure to supersede the value that I have placed on you. You can't allow this gift, sex, to outweigh your value. In fact I paid such a high price for you that nothing else that I've created can replace your worth. So when you open this gift, no man or woman can buy you a car or even a city, they can't pay your light bill, take you around the world, or get your hair or nails done …No, no, no, you can't exchange your self for any of these things, because it does not compare to your value. The exchange value has to be the equivalent; they have to give you their life, for the rest of their life. That's how much you are worth. If they want you and say they really love you, then they have to do what I did, I gave you My life, says the Lord."

> "No one has greater love [no one has shown stronger affection] than to lay down (give up) his own life for his friends." John 15:13 (Amplified)

> "This is how much God loved the world: He gave his Son, his one and only Son. And this is why: so that no one need be destroyed; by believing in him, anyone can have a whole and lasting life." John 3:16 (The Message)

Tragically, there are many of you who have given yourself up so cheaply, merely for a happy meal, a coke and a smile and people continue to come in and get free re-Feels, but they leave you with bill. You are living well beneath your appraised value, and God never wanted it that way. Let's look at His plan for you as described in Genesis 2:18-20 (Amplified):

"Now", the Lord God said, "It is not good (sufficient, satisfactory) that the man should be alone; I will make him a helper meet (suitable, adapted, complementary) for him. And out of the ground the Lord God formed every [wild] beast and living creature of the field and every bird of the air and brought them to Adam to see what he would call them, and whatever Adam called every living creature, that was its name…but for Adam there was not found a helper meet (suitable, adapted, complementary) for him."

For each of us, beginning with Adam, God wanted someone sufficient, suitable, one who would compliment your worth. But some of us are settling and accepting the wild beast! Adam had authority over every other thing that God created because God valued him more than them. Adam named them and the Word says whatever Adam called them, that was its name. After Adam named all the beasts, however, he noticed that none of them compared to him. He said, "Heck, I'm not about to even waste my time. I'm going to sleep." He went to sleep instead of sleeping with the beast! Some of you have been settling for less than you deserve by laying with beast instead of waiting for God's best. You need to do what Adam did. You need to rest and then trust that God will be your backbone and give you someone that compares to what you are worth.

"And the Lord God caused a deep sleep to fall upon Adam; and while he slept, He took one of his ribs or a part of his side and closed up the [place with] flesh. And the rib or part of his side which the Lord God had taken from the man He built up and made into a woman, and He brought her to the man. Then Adam said, This [creature] is now bone of my bones and flesh of my flesh; she shall be called Woman, because she was taken out of a man. Therefore a man shall leave his father and his mother and shall become one flesh. And the man and his wife were both naked and were not embarrassed or ashamed in each other's presence." Genesis 2:21-25 (Amplified)

And this, my friend, is the way that God intended for you. He never wanted you to get naked with anyone until that person gave you their life. Adam didn't settle but waited and trusted God to send him someone suitable and comparable to him. Then he stood at the altar before the Lord and committed himself to this woman by vowing his life to her, "You are now bone of my bone, flesh of my flesh." They united and became one flesh. This man and his wife got naked, made love to one another. And look at what the Word said after they had sex with each other: **they were naked and were not embarrassed or ashamed. They were not embarrassed by feelings of guilt, mortified, discomfited, ashamed or self-conscious or burdened with debt. They were not disconcerted, thrown into disorder or confusion. Neither were they mortified or affected with gangrene (death due to obstructed circulation). Nor were Adam and Eve humiliated**

because of a painful loss of pride, self-respect, or dignity because their union was sanctified by the Lord!

How many of you have felt guilty, humiliated, mortified, disconcerted, ashamed or embarrassed because you had sex with someone you were not married to? If you don't use sex according to God's intended plan for your life, when you get naked, shame **will** attach itself to you. As we discussed in the previous chapter and we also see when Adam had sex with his wife, that whenever you have sex with someone, you become one with that person and whatever they have, you get. You are sleeping with a history. If you get naked but you don't do it in this same order that Adam did, then the results is disorder and confusion in your life. You lose self-respect and pride, and gain a complicated life filled with confusion, and burdened with debt. When you operate in sexual sin you give satan permission to take your hard-earned money and leave you broke. Proverbs 5, verse 10 in the NLT translation says "Strangers will obtain your wealth, and someone else will enjoy the fruit of your labor" when you have illegal sex. Verse 11 continues with, "Afterward you will groan in anguish when disease consumes your body." This can mean a sexually transmitted disease or spiritual gangrene that invades your spirit and cuts off your circulation to God. Physical and spiritual death is then inevitable.

This is why you can't afford to go back to your Ex-boyfriend. Ex is for a reason, it's a thing of the past, good-bye, adios, hasta la vista! So why would you bring it in your future? Why have you allowed your ex-boyfriend satan access back into your life? You had no business leaving Jesus to go back to that fraud anyway but somehow you forgot all the destruction he caused you. You forgot that he almost killed you. You forgot that the temporal pleasure that he gave you nearly cost you your life, but you went back anyway. You got amnesia and didn't remember that it was him who gave you that addiction to men, to women, to sex, masturbation, and pornography; he attached generational curses to you, convinced you to get that abortion.

You let satan blow in your ear and tell you that your life wasn't all that bad when you were with him.

At first, it wasn't working, so he began to taunt you with the painful memories, then he lied to you when he told you that he could make you feel better, to ease the pain, subside your loneliness, and satisfy your sexual need. Well, I'll let you in on something, if satan ever tells you anything, it's a lie! And here are a few of the common lies:

>Lie # 1
>"God does not want you to struggle with your sexual needs so He does not mind that you fulfill them because 'everybody has needs'."
>
>Lie # 2
>The Bible does not say that masturbation is wrong and this is acceptable as long as you don't have sex with anyone else.
>
>Lie # 3
>"There's nothing wrong with oral sex, it's not sex either, just as long as you don't go all the way."

The Truth exposed him for what he really is, "he was a murderer from the beginning and has always hated the truth. There is no truth in him. When he lies, it is consistent with his character; for he is a liar and the father of lies." Let's look at Judges 16:1-3 and see what this lying demon is really trying to do to all of us.

"Now Samson went to Gaza and saw a harlot there, and went in to her. When the Gazites were told, "Samson has come here!" they surrounded the place and lay in wait for him all night at the ate of the city. They were quiet all night, saying, "In the morning, when it is daylight, we will kill him. And Samson lay low till midnight; then he rose at midnight, took hold of the doors of the gate of the city and the two gateposts, pulled them up, bar and all, put them on his shoulders, and carried them at the top of the hill that faces Hebron."

Here you have Samson, a man who was appointed by God to lead Israel, a man of great strength, mighty in battle, raised as a Nazrite from birth to serve the Lord all his life, to abstain from wine or strong drink, to avoid the razor, and to avoid defilement by contact with anything dead. Samson only had one *big* problem- he couldn't stay out of bed with foreign women. Okay, maybe I should have said a HUGE problem. Samson was to avoid contact with the dead, you see, the women he happened to choose were *dead.* The women he was attracted to were uncircumcised Philistines, pagan women who were cut off from God. These women were a hot mess! Hot and on their way to hell and already living hell on earth because satan was their god and they didn't want anything to do with the one and only true God. Yeah, these were the kind of women that this God-fearing man was attracted to. Even though Samson was a chosen man among men, he, too, faced incredible temptation.

So here you have Samson just finished having sex with one of these women, on top of that, she was a prostitute. If not any other better time, Samson's enemies knew that this would be the perfect time to get him-with his pants down. Even his enemies knew his weakness was enticement of women. But Samson laid in the bed with this woman until midnight. Then he got up, seized the doors of the city, lifted them over his shoulders like they were feathers, and was up and out. That was the Ty Adams translation. Now let's pick up the rest of the story in Judges 16:4-5:

"Afterward it happened that he loved a woman in the Valley of Sorek, whose name was Delilah. And the lords of the Philistine came up to her and said to her, "Entice him, and find out where his great strength lies, and by what means we may overpower him, that we may bind him to afflict him; and every one of us will give you eleven hundred pieces of silver."

Samson was clearly controlled by his sexual passions. He certainly had his fair share of foreign women and then he falls in love with Delilah, a greedy gold digger. This cycle of succumbing to his sexual cravings with 'dead' women was Samson's stronghold long before he fell in love with Delilah, but she was to be his demise.

In Judges 14:1-3, Samson's parents were appalled when he told them that he wanted to marry a Philistine woman from the town of Timnah. "Isn't there an acceptable woman among your relatives or among all our people? Must you go to the uncircumcised Philistines to get a wife?" It is evident in Samson's response that he knew what he was doing. His was a conscious decision to deliberately disobey God's command not to intermarry with foreign women and also to neglect God's plan and purpose for his life. It was selfish to only think of himself, knowing that this marriage could ultimately destroy his nation, but it was even worse to blatantly turn against God. "I know she hates God, but she makes me feel good", was Samson's thinking. You would think that he would've learned his lesson after the first time his wife turned on him, but Samson took pleasure in Delilah's seduction and bedroom games.

"So Delilah said to Samson, 'Please tell me where your great strength lies, and with what you may be bound to afflict you.' And Samson said to her, 'If they bind me with seven fresh bowstrings, not yet dried, then I shall become weak, and be like any other man.'" Judges 16:6, 7

It's interesting how some women can know how to manipulate a man into arousal. Here Delilah is seducing Samson by asking him in what way she can take control of him and Samson plays right along with her and tells her, "I'll get weak if you tie me up like this then you can have your way with me, Delilah, and take complete control over me." It goes on to say that the Miss Gold Digger calls up Samson's enemies to say, "I got him, bring the check." His enemies brought the seven fresh bowstrings and Delilah ties Samson up with them. Samson is laying there having a good ole' time, acting as if he is asleep, hoping his little fantasy will be played out. His enemies attempt to get him, but of course Samson's great strength easily breaks free of the strings. Samson was so caught up in this game of seduction that he didn't realize his demise would be caused by his own uncontrolled lust. After this first escapade, Delilah was boiling mad because she realizes that Samson lied to her.

Now, I'm going to ask you what she asked him, "Tell me what you may be bound with." In order for you to ever win the battle of sexual sin, you have to know where your struggle lies. You can not win a battle if you don't know what you are up against. What is your weakness? What is it that you may be bound with? Is it bouts with loneliness? Is it charming men? Is it wicked women? Is it masturbation? Pornography? Homosexuality? Adultery? What are you bound by?

Many single, saved individuals continue to be bound by sexual sin because they will not acknowledge that they struggle. God does not get angry with you because you <u>struggle</u> with sexual sin, but because you won't <u>acknowledge</u> that you are in sin. He tells us in Jeremiah 3:11-13:

"Return, backsliding Israel," says the Lord; 'I will not cause My anger to fall on you. For I am merciful,' says the Lord; 'I will not remain angry forever. Only acknowledge your iniquity, That you have transgressed against the Lord your God."

"Turn back, fickle Israel, I'm not just hanging back to punish you. I'm committed in love to you. My anger doesn't seethe nonstop. Just admit your guilt. Admit your God-defiance. Admit to your promiscuous life with casual partners, pulling strangers into the sex-and religion groves while turning a deaf ear to me.'" God's Decree. "Come back, wandering children!" Jeremiah 3:11-14 (The Message)

Like many of you, Samson would not admit that he struggled with sexual sin and that he was overcome by lust and women. Although Samson had deliberately disobeyed his Nazirite vows and married a Philistine woman, in Judges 15, God displayed His mercy in Samson's life and he was used by God to deliver His people. Yet, Samson still would not acknowledge his sin even though he experienced God's mercy. God's mercy is displayed because that is God's means of redeeming you so that you may acknowledge your sins, to repent and turn away from them so that He can forgive you of them. Not an <u>apology</u>, but <u>repentance</u>. Not to go through the theatrics, cry and apologize because you got caught up and need God to pull you out so you don't have to pay the consequences of your sins.

"Then he became very thirsty; so he cried out to the Lord and said, "You have given this great deliverance by the hand of Your servant; and now shall I die of thirst and fall into the hand of the uncircumcised?" Judges 15:18

God desires true repentance. Mercy does not give you permission to keep on sinning. Don't get it twisted like Samson. Who thought, "Oh, God allowed me to judge Israel even though I was laying up with women, so I don't have to change that." God's mercy was evident in Samson's life even though he married a Philistine woman outside of his own tribe. After this ungodly marriage ended, the Bible says that Samson afterwards had sex with a prostitute and still was able with great strength and anointing to overcome battles with his enemies.

Because Samson did not exercise true repentance, he continued in this lifestyle of sexual sin and then falls in love with another wicked woman, Delilah, as if God is overlooking it. And many of you have not seen the repercussions of your sins, so you continue in them, not realizing that God's mercy is covering you. Just because you get away with freebies with prostitutes, don't think that you can prostitute God's mercy and get away with it. The consequences of your sin may catch up with you before God's mercy does. So was the case with Samson. Here's what happens in Judges 16 verse 15 thru 17:

"Then she said to him, "How can you say, 'I love you', when your heart is not with me? You have mocked me three times, and have not told me where your great strength lies.' And it came to pass, when she pestered him daily with her words and pressed him, so that his soul was vexed to death, that he told her all his heart, and said to her, 'No razor has ever come upon my head, for I have been a Nazirite to God from my mother's womb. If I am shaven, then my strength will leave me, and I shall become weak, and be like any other man."

After Delilah has played in his hair in another attempt to bind Samson up, she comes to find that he has lied to her again. Oh, she is really consumed with anger now so she manipulates him with the famous, "If you love me, you would…" This is the oldest trick in the book and many still fall prey to it. Here's a side note to help some of you: **Real love** would never manipulate someone in to doing something for their benefit at the expense of someone else's hardship. Real love would never force itself on you and twist your arm behind your back or back you in a corner in an effort to get what it wants. Not only did Delilah do this, but she taunted Samson daily until he was vexed to death. She wanted that money bad. Greed had a hold of her in the worst way and satan knew that she would be the perfect person to set Samson up. Here's how this sexual trap ended:

"When Delilah saw that he had told her all his heart, she sent and called for the lords of the Philistines, saying, "Come up once more, for he has told me all his heart." So the lords of the Philistines came up to her and brought the money in their hand. Then she lulled him to sleep on her knees, and she called for a man and had him shave off the seven locks of his head. Then she began to torment him, and his strength left him. And she said, "The Philistines are upon you, Samson!" So he awoke from his sleep, and said, 'I will go out as before, as other times, and shake myself free!' But he did not know that the Lord had departed from him. Then the Philistines took him and put out his eyes, and brought him down to Gaza. They bound him with bronze fetters (chains), and he became a grinder in the prison."

Here is a perfect example of how sexual sin can destroy you. Another prominent issue that I see with both Samson and other Christians who operate in sexual sin is that instead of making a decision that they will denounce sexual sin <u>completely</u>, they attempt to come up with crafty ways to indulge in sin without "crossing the line all the way". Up until this time Samson had constantly yielded to his sexual desires. He begins to see the foreshadowing of judgment coming upon him with constant attacks from his enemies and says within himself, "I need to *slow down* before my wrong catches up with me." *Partial sin is still sin.* "Slowing down" or minimizing your sexual contacts is not the equivalent to living sexually pure.

Samson does not put a complete end to sexual sin but he continues to succumb to sexual perversion by dabbling in it. Samson thought that he could experiment with sex and not "go all the way" with Delilah and continue to operate in the anointing that was on his life. The Bible says that Delilah lulled him to sleep on her knees. The word "lull" means to deceive into trustfulness or to send to sleep with soothing sounds or movements. I am convinced that Delilah deceptively comforted Samson on her knees by performing oral sex on him. This sexual activity with a woman he was not married to cost him his vision! Samson's enemies gouged his eyes out and that's what satan wants to ultimately do to you whom he has convinced that oral sex is not sex and that it's not going "all the way".

Like Samson, satan wants to destroy your vision, your assignment, the very reason why God purposed you. Countless of single people are giving into temptation by dabbling with oral sex, masturbating, looking at pornography, and having sexual intercourse and you are convinced that God is overlooking those sins and that you can continue to show up for mercy believing that you can just apologize when the consequences come up against you. You will find yourself like Samson, thinking that God is still with you, but you'll realize that He's not when you try to shake yourself free. All the other times, Samson was able to get away with fulfilling his sexual desires-or so he thought. But his sins caught up with him. Though he was able to break free from the penalty of sexual sin before, he was not able to shake himself free from its consequences this time. He was so blinded by his sins that he didn't even realize when God was no longer with him.

There are many single Christians living in sexual sin who come to church every Sunday thinking that God is with them because they show up, but attendance does not mean that you and Jesus are tight. There are many Christians who attend church but who are out of relationship with Him. You don't have to have to wear the title of a Christian and bound by sexual sin. You don't have to be part of the statistics. You don't have to be chained to your past, and held captive to sin by satan's traps.

How do you break free from the enemy's trap? How do you prevent from falling into the same situation as Samson and losing your God-given vision? How do you finally shake free from your sexual struggle? Psalms 32:5 declares:

"I acknowledged my sin to You, and my iniquity I did not hide. I said, I will confess my transgressions to the Lord [continually unfolding the past till all is told]--then You [instantly] forgave me the guilt and iniquity of my sin. Selah [pause, and calmly think of that]!"

Are you ready to come face to face with your struggle? Then acknowledge to the Lord that you struggle with sexual sin so that God can forgive you of those sins and ultimately deliver and heal you of them. Not just partially, but completely. I remember when my niece, Promise who twelve years old at the time, was eating candy in church and I told her two consecutive times to put it away until we got home. On the way home, after reprimanding her, I told her that she could now eat the candy. She responded, "I threw it away. You had to tell me twice not to eat it in church. It's not that I didn't listen to you the first time, but the second time, I put it in my mouth because I gave in to temptation and before I knew it, it was in my mouth without me even thinking about it. When I realized that I had it back in my mouth, I took it and threw it away. From now on, I'm getting rid of stuff and throwing away anything that tempts me or causes me to be disobedient to you and God." My mouth was sprung open and my eyebrows raised; I was shocked and amazed, but learned a valuable lesson from a 12-year-old.

Many of you have allowed temptation-even those like music, movies, TV- to subconsciously become your **cheap thrills**. I had a friend, named Eric, who was a God-fearing man, solid in his affairs and work relations—just a well-put-together person. Every time I would hear from him, you would hear the TV going in the background. Whenever he came home, the first thing he would do is turn the TV on and it would stay on all night. He watched TV extensively.

One particular day, I brought it to his attention. Laughing, I said, "Do you know that you have a TV demon?" After laughing, he said, "Come to think of it, you are right. I didn't even realize that I was doing it but the reason I do it is because I don't have a wife or kids. To be honest with you, I use it as a comfort and if I turn it off, I'll realize that I'm here by myself." I responded, "Well, why don't you try filling that space with something else?"

That would be hard for some of you, seeing as though you use these arenas to comfort and pacify, to occupy your time, because you wouldn't know what to do with yourself if you turned them off. So you use them to turn you on. You are substituting it for the "real thing." These arenas are just cheap thrills. A cheap thrill is anything artificial that makes you feel good, excite or pacify you, or gives you a quick high at a cheap or low cost. What is in your life that makes you feel good temporarily? What occupies your time that cost you no effort at all to get? What gives you a quick instant feel-good but after it is gone, leaves you feeling empty?

In order to receive your sexual deliverance **and** maintain it, this is what has to happen: you need to be honest about where you are at. One of the things I see with Christians is that they are afraid to talk to God about their feelings . . . about what makes them feel good. Have you ever said, "Lord, I'm really missing sex, I'm really in the mood"? Some of you are shaking in your pants at the thought of saying that to Him. He already knows what is in your heart and what's on your mind and the things you did that no one else knows. He knows your hidden faults and secrets; He's just waiting for your permission to talk about it.

The other thing you need to do is: know your weakness. What are your struggles? Some of you don't know or have not yet recognized what that is. Some of you play it off like you don't know or you are in denial. This is one of the easiest avenues for satan to come in so that he can tempt you. Some of you men will sit right in front of the TV and watch a naked woman, and you know that you can't handle that. You have to **constantly guard your soul** because satan is waiting for the opportunity to trip you up and he'll use you to do that.

I've never had a problem with tithing. I didn't take God's money and go buy myself a dress with my tithe or pay my cell phone bill with it. I did not have a problem with going to mid-week Bible study. That was not my issue. Oh, I would make it to church, but I was probably in some man's arms before I got there. My struggle was sex. So, at all costs, I had to remove anything and everything that contributed to my addiction. I changed my phone number. My body was too weak to tell him no when he called. That deep raspy voice spoke to my weak flesh every time. I threw away CDs that aroused my sexual drive and any music that reminded me of "Mike and Kenny." Every time I turned on "I don't see nothin' wrong with a li'l bump and grind," I was bumping and grinding. Why? Because I rehearsed in my mind that nothing was wrong with a little sex. A little or a lot, one bed partner or five, it's wrong if you are not married.

I knew I was weak in this area, there was no denying it,

even though, sometimes, I did deny it. I got fed up with falling for the same old tricks and allowing satan to use me, to set me up. I got honest with myself and said, *"Ty, satan is not your problem. You are. You continue to do the same things that get you in the same beds. You will continue to battle with sexual sin until you make up your mind that you have to let some old habits go. You give satan permission to trip you up because you will not let go of things that tempt you."* Stop blaming the devil every time you have sex because he does not have any power until you release it to him. Get fed up with sexual sin, get tired of falling into traps, stop making it okay to dabble. Take the power back and use it to overcome.

If you do not take the responsibility of guarding what enters into you, you will become subject to lasciviousness (uncontrollable lust). It's those small things, those small foxes that destroy you. This is where the set-up comes in; satan will not abruptly throw a woman into your lap, no, he tries to be smoother than that, my brothers. The first thing he'll do is watch you and set you up by planting seemingly innocent things early in the game. He'll let you repeatedly—night after night—sit there and watch naked women on TV and listen to music that talks about bumping and grinding. Right when your sexual drive is at its peak, he'll make sure she calls you at eleven o'clock at night, "Hey, what are you doing? I was just thinking about you; I didn't call for any particular reason. I was **just** in the neighborhood and **just** wanted to say hi. Can I **just** stop by for a minute?" Yeah, right, just in the neighborhood at 11. Then, your naïve, silly self answers, "Yeah, **just** for a minute, come on by." Don't you know that the only thing open late is drive-thrus and legs?! Now, you're singing a sad ole song again, "It's morning and we've slept the night away."

Knowing your weaknesses and getting control of them, places you ahead of satan and can prevent him from using them against you. In order to maintain control you need to constantly take inventory of your life.

"...Let us lay aside every weight, and the sin which so easily ensnares us, and let us run with endurance the race that is set before us, looking unto Jesus, the author and finisher of our faith." Hebrews 12:1b-2a

There may be some things in your life that you believe are not sins, but they could very well be a "weight." You may look at these things in your life as minute and trivial, but the Bible says that weight and sin easily takes you off-track: they easily tangle and twist you up. Every temptation, every person in your life, is either moving you towards God or taking you away from Him. Now, in order to appropriately take inventory and decide if something is supposed to be in your life or not, if it's a weight or sin, you have to look unto Jesus to determine it.

You probably think that you are okay and you have your issues under control. Good, this is for you, then. Comparing this to the physical state of your health, you would go to visit your doctor for regular check-ups even when there are no signs of sickness. They call these well visits. The purpose of these well visits are to detect any signs of failing health at an early stage or to prevent sickness altogether. Though you may not see any evident signs of sexual sin or weights, you need to see Jesus for a check-up.

Back in the day they would use a chastity belt to lock a young woman, to prevent her from having sex. No, I am not going to tell you to put a chastity belt on your overgrown self! You would just simply let him take it off. Before you leave from your check-up appointment, I'm going to make sure that you'll get some chastity tablets. No, not birth control pills! Why are some of you single, Christian women taking birth control pills, anyway, and why are you, single men, carrying condoms? You are planning to fail. You cannot plan to overcome and fail at the same time. You can not have a "just in case I fall" plan. If you are taking birth control pills or carrying condoms, the first thing that you need to do is throw them away. You cannot grab a hold to a future of celibacy with a grip on your sinful past. If you plan to fail, you will fail. Plan to overcome instead.

I had a male friend who was in the navy for several years and we had a discussion about how he was able to sustain himself while he was at sea. He said, "Well, our commander was adamant about keeping a ship full of men focused so they gave us something called Salt Peter. Salt Peter was used to keep our sex drives down so that we could keep our attention on the duties at hand and not on sex." To maintain your focus and to keep you from engaging in sexual activities, Doctor Jesus recommends "Salt Peter." Here's what your prescription contains:

Salt is good, it preserves, seasons and flavors.

Good: morally excellent, well-behaved; worthy, not a counterfeit, spoiled or tainted

Preserve: keeps up or maintains; to resist decomposition (to rot, corrupt, decay, decline from excellence) or fermentation (an uneasy state of mind or to agitate or excite the feelings, desires, or passions)

Season/Flavor: a distinctive quality or feature; the most important or main attraction

You are salt and are made up of these elements. You possess the ingredients to maintain purity, to withstand decay. You are not tainted, but worthy and morally excellent. You have distinctive qualities that stand out from other people and you have control of your feelings and desires. But where do counterfeit Christians come from? They lose their flavor. They are missing the most important part.

> "You are the salt of the earth; but if the salt loses its flavor, how shall it be seasoned? It is then good for nothing but to be thrown out and trampled underfoot by men." Matthew 5:13

> "For everyone will be seasoned with fire, and every sacrifice will be seasoned with salt." Mark 9:49

Salt (you) will not get your seasoning, your flavor until you sacrifice yourself. The sacrifice (you) has to have a broken spirit and a contrite heart (sincerely remorseful). This does not mean that you are sorry that you got caught, but that you sincerely acknowledge that your life is without substance outside of Him. You recognize that your spirit is bankrupt without Him and the lifestyle that you live is contrary to God's will, and then you repent/turn away from that life and turn to Him.

Salt has to be free from impurities and every sacrifice has to go through the fire. You will not be purified (the main attraction) until you go through the fire. What are you still holding on to? What do you have that you are not letting go? What is it that you consider to be more valuable than Jesus? Whatever it is, it's standing in the place of purity.

To sacrifice is to the surrender of something of value for the sake of something else; to sell at a loss. You need to realize that going through the refining fire is inevitable. This is the process in which you sell yourself out to Jesus for the loss of fleshly pleasures and sin. It is the only way that you can get to a pure state; some things have to be burned off of you. This is where the residue comes off, the counterfeit spirits and the contamination. The fingerprints, the scarring and tearing of your spirit, the guilt and the shame will be destroyed and consumed in the fire. When fire cannot destroy something, it purifies it. The only thing left will be you.

Chapter 3 Committing Adultery

"I promised your hand in marriage to Christ, presented you as a virgin to her husband. And now I'm afraid that exactly as the Snake seduced Eve with his smooth patter, you are being lured away from the simple purity of your love for Christ." II Corinthians 11:2-3 (The Message)

I remember when the movie *Indecent Proposal* came out and the debatable question was asked: "Would you sleep with someone for one night for a million dollars?" Many of you would take the money without thinking. Oh, you wouldn't? Well, how much could someone pay you to cheat on God? If you're single and having sex, you're cheating on Him now *without* the money. I don't have to use my imagination to see what you might do if a million was on the table.

Many proposals were offered to me and I cheated on God, again and again. Man after man, bed after bed, one relationship after another. Do you want to know the name of the woman at the well in John 4:7? Ty. I was the woman with the many boyfriends-made-husbands. I was thirsty and none of my lovers quenched my thirst. I used sexual relationships to cover up the emptiness inside of me that had built up from childhood. I was damaged as a child by the hands of men who violated and sexually molested me. I was heavily exposed to homosexuality, incestuous relationships, and sexual perversion.

At the age of 13, my virginity was unlawfully and prematurely taken by a man seven years older than me. My mind was plagued heavily with thoughts of those who illegally tampered with my body. Not to mention, I was crushed and devastated when I found out that a relative allowed her 11-year-old child to be the victim of a perverted fantasy. This relative would perform any requested sexual acts with a man for money. She came up short when his fantasy was to have a virgin. Of course, she couldn't honor that request, and so she gave her 11-year-old daughter to him. This and many other sexual perversions among close relatives continued to haunt me my entire teenage years. I was disgusted and I vowed I wouldn't live the life of some of my family members . . . not knowing that I was already starting to live it.

Sexual promiscuity became my way of life. I was trained to believe that sex was just as common as breathing. There was no restraint exercised on my part. After a while, I began to blame it on a high sex drive. (Any excuse will do.) I became so enslaved to my sins that sex became a pattern independent of my conscious mind. In other words, I didn't think; I just did it.

I began covering up emotional pain and brokenness with a greater level of promiscuity. I fooled myself into believing that "the more men, the merrier" was a way of me having sexual control over my life, since it was taken away from me at such a young age. Men would no longer take advantage of me; I now I have the control over them. But the more I ran in to hotels, the greater the quest for fulfillment grew and before I knew it, I became what I was once ashamed of and hated so much. One day of the forbidden turned into years of sexual entrapment. For a moment, I was having fun with sin until the knock on the door of my heart grew increasingly louder.

"Behold, I stand at the door, and knock: if any man hear my voice, and open the door, I will come in to him, and will sup with him, and he with me." Revelations 3:20

I knew who was at the door, so I opened it just a little and I started to periodically go to church. I accepted Jesus in my life as Savior, but I didn't allow Him to become Lord. I would go to church on Sunday, but I would go back home to sin on Sunday night. I knew I didn't want to go to hell, so I accepted Jesus, but I had no intentions of giving up my sex life. God was only evident in my life on Sunday mornings between the hours of 11 A.M. and 2 P.M. Until one day I was forced to see who I was in the mirror.

One Saturday night around ten, a friend (we'll call her Lynn) came by the house. Lynn was shocked to see me in my pj's and a floral silk scarf on my head. Usually, I would be in a pair of high-heeled shoes and a tight-fitted dress on my way out the door to the bar.

"What are you doing in your pajamas? You're not going out?" Lynn asked.

Yawning, I answered, "No, I gotta get up for church in the morning."

"Church? How do you do that?" she looked at me strangely as if she did not recognize the person standing in front of her.

Clueless, I responded, "Do what?"

"Ah, go to church and live the life that you live. You were just out with me last week," Lynn said sarcastically. Lynn had also traveled the road of lesbianism. She left her husband and kids and became a "dancer." No, not ballet, but striptease dancing. I answered her, "Well, how else am I supposed to get myself together . . ."

She interrupted me, "You are a hypocrite! I used to go to church. My father was the assistant pastor. I know the Word. The Bible says that God would rather you be hot or cold. You are lukewarm!"

> "I know all the things you do, that you are neither hot nor cold. I wish you were one or the other! But since you are like lukewarm water, I will spit you out of my mouth!" Revelations 3:15, 16 (NLT)

Both of us were so angry we were about to cut each other's throat. "Well, if you know the Bible so well," I said, "why don't you *live it?*"

Rolling her neck, Lynn said, "Because I ain't fake like you!"

I was appalled! "Fake?! At least I didn't turn my back on God so that I could marry satan and live a hellish lifestyle forever after!" Just before I was about to punch Lynn, my friend, with whom I was living in sin, came in and broke up our catfight.

I was sooooo mad! I couldn't believe her. The audacity! Then, I channeled my anger over to God. I ran in the bathroom and fell on the floor, crying hysterically, *"Is this how you see me? Is this how you really look at me, like I'm lukewarm? Well, I can't help it. I'm trying, but I don't know how to change, I don't know how to stop living the way I'm living and if You don't like it, you're going to have to change me. I can't, I don't know how to . . ."* I just lay there on the floor, crying all night. The next morning's sunlight in my eyes woke me and I heard a gentle voice say, "Wake up, it's time for you to go to church." I was surprised. After I just hollered at God, I didn't think I would see daylight; I thought I would be dead. But then I remembered Romans 2:4:

> Don't you realize how kind, tolerant, and patient God is with you? Or don't you care? Can't you see how kind he has been in giving you time to turn from your sin? (NLT)

That was when I realized that I had been committing adultery. Spiritual adultery. I was lukewarm and I was cheating on the One who had always been faithful to me. My sin left me feeling dirty and ashamed. It was shocking to me that God continued pulling on me. You may feel that your situation is hopeless and that the Lord has given up on you. I thought He wanted to punish me for my sin and send me straight to hell after spitting me out of His mouth. I had misinterpreted Revelations 3:16 because the Lord spoke to me clearly and said, "I don't care how bad you've messed things up. I don't care how dirty you've gotten. You are not beyond repair because even when I spit on 'dirt' I can perform a miracle in your life and you'll never be the same!"

"Some people brought a sightless man and begged Jesus to give him a healing touch. Taking him by the hand, he led him out of the village. He put spit in the man's eyes…So Jesus laid hands on his eyes again. The man looked hard and realized that he had recovered perfect sight, saw everything in bright, twenty-twenty focus." Mark 8:22b-23, 25 (The Message)

God maintained His position, He never changed. He consistently loved me while I was in my mess. That's why I love Him. I'll never forget that day. My life then took a series of turns. I was never the same. I begin to see things for what they really were. The desires that I had for sin began to aggravate me. The bar scenes even began to make me sick to my stomach and I wanted a way out more than ever. But satan and his stronghold didn't want to let me go and I was feeling confused. *"I don't want to be here anymore, but I can't see my way out. You've been in it too long, Ty. You just can't get up and go like that. Where will you go, what will you do? . . . but you have to go . . . but I can't go, I'm scared. This is too big of a change. This step is too big for me to climb. I'll just gradually get out of it. No, I can't do this, I don't want to make a decision . . ."*

Suddenly, all the thoughts that ran through my head ceased when the Lord spoke and said, "Are you choosing this lifestyle over me?" Tears began to fill my eyes and trickle down the sides of my face as I pictured me standing at the Gates on Judgment Day trying to get in. Disheartened by the sad look on His face because He had to turn me away, before I could swallow or blink an eye, I answered, "No. I choose You." Without any further hesitation, I picked up the phone and called this woman who I was living in sin with and said, "I'm not coming back. I can't . . . I can't choose you over Jesus."

I was without excuse. I had seen God's hand move in my life. I personally encountered mercy face to face. I experienced and tasted grace and I was given chance after chance, yet, I chose to compromise. I lived a double life: on Sunday I would spend time with God and the next day I would hook up with satan. I knew God's goodness, I knew His faithfulness and commitment to me, but I was prostituting the gifts and the blessings. I soon realized that standing in the middle of the street, I would eventually get hit by a moving vehicle full of consequences. The following passage from Romans 1:18 through verse 32 illustrates my life at that point in time:

"But God shows his anger from heaven against all sinful, wicked people who push the truth away from themselves. For the truth about God is known to them instinctively. God has put this knowledge in their hearts. From the time the world was created, people have seen the earth and sky and all that God made. They can clearly see his invisible qualities--his eternal power and divine nature. So they have no excuse whatsoever for not knowing God. Yes, they knew God, but they wouldn't worship Him as God or even give Him thanks. And they began to think up foolish ideas of what God was like. The result was that their minds became dark and confused . . .

So God let them go ahead and do whatever shameful things their hearts desired. As a result, they did vile and degrading things with each other's bodies. Instead of believing what they knew was the truth about God, they deliberately chose to believe lies. So they worshiped the things God made but not the Creator himself, who is to be praised forever. Amen. That is why God abandoned them to their shameful desires.

Even the women turned against the natural way to have sex and instead indulged in sex with each other. And the men, instead of having normal sexual relationships with women, burned with lust for each other. Men did shameful things with other men and, as a result, suffered within themselves the penalty they so richly deserved. When they refused to acknowledge God, He abandoned them to their evil minds and let them do things that should never be done . . . They are fully aware of God's death penalty for those who do these things, yet they go right ahead and do them anyway. And, worse yet, they encourage others to do them, too."

I was living an unnatural life deserving death. A wicked and sinful mind does not have the ability to know or serve God, because it has chosen to ignore God's truth concerning your life.

God says that you'll be without excuse, for He has shown Himself to you. He has also shown you that He does not approve of this kind of lifestyle. God will not override your will. He has laid out His plan for you in the Bible and will allow you to decide if you want to live it or not. But know this: attached to those choices are consequences. Understand, God does not send anyone to hell, **your choices do**.

Though I didn't verbally say that I choose satan, my life did. Not choosing to serve God completely and wholeheartedly is a choice made automatically to serve satan. Standing in the middle of the road compromising does not make you exempt. There is no middle ground, because God does not do ménage a trois. You are either for God or for satan and when you stand in the middle, you automatically, by default, choose satan. It didn't mean anything that I was going to church because satan was my lord and I was dying a slow death.

"Have mercy on me, O Lord, for I am in trouble; My eyes wastes away with grief, Yes my soul and body! For my life is spent with grief, And my years with sighing; My strength fails because of my iniquity, And my bones waste away." Psalms 31:10

I was in anguish. The pleasures of sin had ended because the effects of that sin outweighed it. I was buried beneath the consequences. But even though I was leaving death, it seemed as if it was the hardest thing to do. The torment of sin wouldn't let me sleep. I would often lay curled up in a knot in the floor all night crying. I read Isaiah 59:1, 2:

"Behold, the Lord's hand is not shortened that it can not save; nor His ear heavy, that it cannot hear. But your iniquities have separated you from your God; and your sins have hidden His face from you, so that He will not hear."

God wanted to save me, but it was still up to me to let Him. God has given everyone of us the power to decide. He loves us so much that He did not take our free will; you have the choice of living for Him. He did not want robots He could command to love Him.

I made a decision to live completely for the Lord, not knowing I was pregnant. Right before I made the decision, in stupidity, I fell for Mr. Tall, Fiiiiiiiiiine, and Charming. Did I say charming? He had charisma oozing outta' his ears and before I knew it, he had me pinned underneath his covers—just like a sly ole devil.

Then I had a "too late" experience. I realized after I slept with him that I was only jumping from one sin to another. So I came to my senses, immediately ended the relationship, repented, and said, "Lord, You didn't deliver me from hell to go back to it. I messed up, I fell, but I honestly say to you, Lord, I really want to live my life right for you." Just as He always does, He forgave me. I had major plans to live my life totally for Him and I had purposed in my heart that not only would my mouth, but my life would give evidence to my commitment to Him, until . . . A month rolled around and the cycle that repeated itself for the last 12 years of my life was interrupted by life . . . I was pregnant.

How could this be! I was so devastated! I cried and I cried and I cried. I can't have this baby! *"Lord, do you know I carry a Bible? The usher and ministers that see me every Sunday and Wednesday will notice my belly expanding with no ring on my finger, and there's no "I do" in sight . . . and what will all the people who just heard me say out of my mouth that I'm a committed Christian, going to think? I can't have this baby, Lord, I can't. What is my family going to think? . . . I can hear them now, 'I knew she was fake!'"*

God answered: "What am *I* going to think? You didn't give life and you can't take it away. You can't cover up your mistakes by layering it with sin. You can't cover up your mistakes—that's My job. This baby you have in you is not a mistake. I will not cover up this baby but I will cover the sin you committed. I'll cover it up and I'll treat you as if it never happened. You have proclaimed Me as Lord, now trust Me to be that for you and this child." I picked up the phone and called the abortion clinic and canceled my appointment.

Some people believe that a person's existence begins after 9 months of pregnancy when the mother delivers. Some people believe that existence starts at conception. Both are farthest from the truth. Before you were an embryo in your mother's womb, God held you. Before the foundation of the world, God carefully crafted you.

> "You made all the delicate, inner parts of my body and knit me together in my mother's womb. Thank you for making me so wonderfully complex! Your workmanship is marvelous--and how well I know it. You watched me as I was being formed in utter seclusion, as I was woven together in the dark of the womb. You saw me before I was born. Every day of my life was recorded in your book. Every moment was laid out before a single day had passed." Psalms 139:13-16 (NLT)

When conception takes place, it's God's hand that does it; it's pre-planned, on purpose even if <u>you</u> didn't plan it. God breathes life into every child. The sin could have been a mistake, but not the baby.

A baby should not have to pay for its parent's mistakes with its life.

- In the United States an abortion is performed every twenty-two seconds; (CDC)
- more than 4,000 abortions will be performed today (CDC, Right to Life)

- Three in four women say they had abortions for reasons of inconvenience. Stats from the Alan Guttmacher Institute (1992)
- The Elliott Institute reports that approximately 40 percent of all abortion cases involve coercion, usually from boyfriends.

The leading cause of death among African Americans is not crime, not cancer not AIDS, but abortions. (Right To Life)

At conception, sperm joins ovum to form a single cell which, miraculously, contains the genetic blueprint for every detail of development: sex, hair and eye color, height, skin, tone, and more. Over the next week this tiny human being, consisting of several hundred cells, travels through the fallopian tube to the uterus, implanting in the nutrient-rich lining. Within 22 days the heart is beating and the spinal column, nervous system, kidneys, liver and digestive tract take shape. Within few short weeks the baby is ¼ inch long: already ten thousand times larger than when he/she began. By 40 days brain waves may be recorded. Facial features take shape: ears, nose, lips, tongue, and even tiny teeth. By 8 weeks all body systems are present and from then on the changes are mainly in size and refinement of body parts are already developed.

Babies are **never** a mistake, never! I don't care what the circumstances are and how much of a mess you've gotten yourself into, God stands ready to forgive you and is both willing and able to restore and deliver you. God can turn any situation around and He's able to do that because Mary didn't abort Jesus. In Matthew 1:18-25 you can see that Mary could have used the excuse that she wasn't married to Joseph yet and could have secretly gone to the abortion clinic; then hell would be home for both you and me. Mary's decision not to abort Jesus, our Redeemer, obligates God to forgive and redeem you. Don't take the life of your own child; God took the life of His own child so that you wouldn't have to. God is not condemning you, He wants to deliver you. Let Him. I could have terminated my pregnancy with my daughter Heaven, but I *chose* to receive God's forgiveness. I was trying to help God by proving to other people that I was delivered from my sexual sins, instead of letting Him prove it through the supernatural change that was taking place in my life.

I found myself a victim of a generational curse. This is defined as an evil or misfortune that has been invoked upon a person through his/her family. When you have gone to the doctor, at one time or another, he has asked you a series of questions like, "Does high blood pressure run in your family? Sickle cell? Cancer?" Generational physical ailments are the same as generational spiritual ailments or curses. Let's do a spiritual check. Does sexual immorality run in your family? Out-of-wedlock pregnancy? Homosexuality? Incest, molestation, abortions, adultery? Pornography? Fornication?

If you answered yes to any of these, a generational curse could have passed itself on to you. I found myself patterning after a number of family members and close friends. This is one reason why you have to be careful as to who you allow yourself and your children to associate with even family. Spirits transfer; you become your environment. You mirror the person you accompany yourself with. I've seen three or four generations of alcoholism, molestation, unwedlock pregnancies, and incestuous relationships. But God has provided a means for you to be delivered and set free. Your life can begin to reflect the life of Christ. You do not have to die in your sin, whether generational or by choice. Don't be an accomplice in your own victimization!

"Do you think, asks the Sovereign LORD, that I like to see wicked people die? Of course not! I only want them to turn from their wicked ways and live." Ezekiel 18:23 (NLT)

"To the pure [in heart and conscience] all things are pure, but to the defiled and corrupt and unbelieving nothing is pure; their very minds and consciences are defiled and polluted. They profess to know God [to recognize, perceive, and be acquainted with Him], but deny and disown and renounce Him by what they do; they are detestable and loathsome, unbelieving and disobedient and disloyal and rebellious, and [they are] unfit and worthless for good work (deed or enterprise) of any kind." Titus 1:15, 16 (Amplified)

You can't continue to play the field by singing in the choir and shacking up. You cannot pay your tithes, preach a sermon, shout and run down the aisle and go back home to sin. You can't be the minister of music or a gospel recording artist and live in sexual immorality—heterosexual or homosexual, from the pew to the pulpit, man or woman, Romans 2:11 states that there is no partiality with God. It's shameful and a disgrace to see ministers or men and women of the cloth sleeping around. You are expected to feed God's people, not sleep with them!

"But, Lord, people were worshipping to the music that I recorded. They were at the concerts crying and lifting their hands. They received salvation after I preached my sermons." As indicated in Luke 13:27, the Lord's response to that will be, "Depart from me, you workers of iniquity, you who practice and live in sin." We don't need another Judas in the camp. Don't continue to kiss Jesus on the cheek and then betray Him by lying in sin. I don't care how many times you go to church each week, how many Scriptures you know, how many sermons you've preached, or altar calls you've led. Don't think for one minute that because you can sing and you top the chart or the congregation stands when the choir gets up, that your active sexual lifestyle is disregarded or ignored. God can not use a dirty vessel.

Just because you operate in your gift, just because God uses your gift doesn't mean that He is overlooking your sin. You can be used if you are in the way. God will use your gift to bless His people, and you can still bust hell wide open. The gifts and callings are without repentance. There will not be a recall on what God gives you, so just because your gift is used does not mean you are right in how you are living and you are in good terms with Him. Don't get to the Gate and get turned away.

Brothers, don't think because you sneak out the church and go and commit sexual acts with a "worldly woman," that no one will find out. Your sin will turn on you and expose you.

> But if you do not do so (obey God), then take note, you have sinned against the Lord; and be sure your sin will find you out. Numbers 32:33 (Amplified)

And there are a lot of you "sanctified brothas" who will not have sex with someone in your church, but you'll go and get a woman who can't even tell you where Genesis is in the Bible, believing that you'll get away with it. Did you forget that you became one with her? You become a harlot when you lie with a harlot. I guarantee you, though, that if you walk away from her and join back up with the Lord, the Bible declares in I Corinthians 6:16, 17 that you'll be delivered of that bond with her and become one with Him again.

Even though sin can entangle and overthrow you, sin is no match for God. Romans 5:20 emphatically states that "Where sin abounds, grace abounds much more!" I don't care how long you've been in your mess, how bad it is, and how many times you fell and went back, God's grace outweighs it all! God's grace is not in competition with your sin. Grace will win over sin every time. It's God's grace that has delayed and interrupted sin's fatal destruction in your life. You know that you should have been wiped out, but God was longsuffering with you because He had faith that you would turn away from sin and run to Him. Come to your senses. Leave that life of destruction, and accept His mercy.

I know you have heard this many times, "You've made your bed in hell, now lie in it," but God is not like man. I know people have given you this false misconception of God, but the high cost He paid and His unconditional love for you makes it impossible for Him to give up on you so easily like man does. Though He hates sin, He looks at you in your worst mess, looks at you in your hell-bound life and reaches right down and grabs you out of it.

> "Where can I go from Your Spirit? Or where can I flee from Your presence? If I ascend into heaven, You are there; If I make my bed in hell, behold, You are there. Even there your hand shall lead me, and Your right hand shall hold me." Psalms 139:7, 8

You can't hide or run from God because of your sin; His love won't let you. You think He's looking for you to send you to hell when He's trying to pull you out of it! I know for some of you, it may seem far off and it's almost impossible, but with God, all things are possible! The reason you don't see it is because of the <u>stronghold</u> of sin. **A stronghold is a mindset impregnated with hopelessness that causes the believer to accept as unchangeable something that he/she knows is contrary to the will of God.**

You know homosexuality is wrong, a sin, and contrary to the will of God. You know that sex outside of marriage is sin and not God's will. You know that masturbation and pornography is not God's will and is a sin. Some of you, men, have given up altogether and have even stopped trying to live a holy life and refrain from sex. You have used the excuse that celibacy and sexual abstinence is for the "religious women" of the church. Let's look at an email that I received from a 31 year-old man, you'll find my response to him in the FAQ section at the end of this book:

> "I wanted to know what do you do when you feel like you have to release the sperms in your body? Outside of having sexual intercourse, the only way is through masturbation but you said that masturbation is a sin. I also spoke with some people and they told me that there comes a point in a man's life when you just have to release it. Otherwise, it will hurt you and they said that it's proven medically. Many people say that it's impossible for a man to refrain from having sex. So, I need some clarity on that if you don't mind." Mr. H.Y

This email mirrors the thinking of many men who believe that it's impossible for a single man to live sexually pure, like this young man named Mike I know who believed that a man was not a man unless he had several women to have sex with at any time. He prided himself on his good looks and charm and he could be seen around town any night of the week with a different woman. Mike's male friends envied him, but in view of God's standards, Tom was not a *real* man, but a wimp! A wimp who lacked self-control and, since he lacked control, he twisted the truth and walked around as an imposter by sticking the word "man" on his chest. The stronghold of sin had him believe that there was no chance of living a sexually pure life as a single man. Sin blinded Mike of God's power to deliver him so he remained in his sin even though he knew that it was in direct opposition and conflict with God's will. **Never make what's wrong, right in your mind. A real man walks away from something he strongly desires, to please the God whom he really loves.**

You need to make up in your mind that you want to be delivered like David and you're going to do whatever to get it. King David became a victim of his sexual addiction and his passion for women when he committed adultery and had sex with a married woman and got her pregnant; yet he repented and became the greatest king over Israel and in Acts 13:22 God declared him a man after His own heart.

> "Then David confessed to Nathan, 'I have sinned against the LORD.' Nathan replied, 'Yes, but the LORD has forgiven you, and you won't die for this sin.'"
> II Samuel 12:13 (The Message)

You don't have to settle for bondage. God has a purpose and a plan for your life and you do not need to settle for less. He does not care how long you've been in sin, how many women or men you've slept with. Suicide is not your option or your answer, God Is. Self-inflicted tragedy will, undoubtedly, prematurely terminate God's plan. Your past does not cancel out your future. Neither can it cancel God's purpose for your life. Your life, your purpose for existence, and your ministry are not over. **Your past does not determine if you are capable of possessing your future. In fact, it proves that you are qualified for it.**

The Samaritan woman who had sexual affairs with several men who she was not married to, we find in John 4:29 and 39 she became a living witness for Jesus; a whoremonger turned into an evangelist. Only Jesus can take a sex-crazed man and woman, bound by lust, and make them pure and elevate them at the same time. That's the problem—folks walking around as if they have been saved all their life, while you walk around in shame, believing that you're the only one struggling with sexual sin.

Everybody has a past, everybody is not telling it, though, because satan does not want you to believe that Jesus is still delivering his people from sexual sin. That loser, satan, does not want you or anyone else to overcome so he puts God's people in a position where they are sworn to a secret—the secret that Jesus delivers. I had to share my testimony with you so that you would know that Jesus still delivers because Revelations 12:11 declares that when I testify you over come your struggle. And when Jesus set you free, you are free indeed!

You too can be restored. You can get back to God's original intent for your life: **a single, pure virgin.** That sounds impossible for some of you, but the truth is, you can become a virgin again. How? Covenant. When I was a kid I had friends that I was really close to and enjoyed their friendship so much that we would share all our secrets. We wanted to be the best of friends forever, like sisters, and never, ever part, so we entered into a pact. We would prick each other's finger with a needle 'til blood came out. Then, we would cross our fingers where the blood would touch and say, "Now, we are blood sisters." This was our covenant- our way of promising each other that we'd be friends no matter what. "You've got my back, I've got yours. Whatever I have, you have."

Whoever you had sexual intercourse with, you did the same thing—you entered into a covenant with them. When your virginity was taken, blood was shed, and you entered a covenant with that person. Now, in order to regain your sexual purity, you have to enter into a covenant with Jesus. The Blood has already been shed and the promises have already been fulfilled and now all you have to do according to Romans 11:27 is enter into a covenant with Him. Then, virginity can be restored because the blood covenant you enter into with God contains wholeness and purity and it will take away all your sins. You swap. God takes your mess—your sin—and He gives you purity in exchange. He'll close the external orifice back up and cause you to become a virgin again.

I know some Pharisee spirits in the church are mad at me now. That's the reason why some of you left the church or are afraid to come in—there are some people who have made you believe that you are a hypocrite in church because you're struggling with sexual sin. Let's look at what Jesus does to people who struggle with sexual immorality. Jesus is at your church, preaching a message, and here comes the deacons interrupting the service. Here, you have the scribes and Pharisees in John 8:1-12 bringing this woman to Jesus who they caught in adultery and they said, "Teacher, this woman was caught in the very act.[29] Now, the law commands that such be stoned, but what do You say?" They were trying to trip Jesus up by placing Him in a position where He had to choose between his loyalty to the law and his loyalty to those who violated the law. The next sentence said, "But Jesus ..."

I know, just like this woman, and just like me, you deserved death. You deserved to be stoned for your sins. We cheated on God, walked away and betrayed Him and the law stated that the sexual sins that we've committed were only payable by death . . . but Jesus! Ignoring them, He stoops down and writes on the ground with His finger . . . He interrupted death. Jesus knelt down and began to blot out her sins, my sins, your sins. He wiped out the law; He wiped out the requirements that sentenced us to the death penalty, just as He promised in Colossians 2:14. He then stood up and said, "He who is without sin cast the first stone." Fully knowing that they all deserved death, Jesus stood alone with the woman and asked, "Where are your accusers?" Jesus, who was without sin, had every right to stone her, yet He forgave her, "Neither do I condemn you, go and sin no more."

The scribes and Pharisees thought the fate for this woman was going to be death. But they took her to the right person, into the church where Jesus was. Sick people go to hospitals; sinners go to church. If you have a sin problem, you don't run from the church, you run into it. Let me let you in on something: they don't have it altogether themselves, either. Trust me, God is dealing with them about something. Church is not a place for "people who've got it together." It's for people like you and me, who need to maintain deliverance to strengthen ourselves and our relationship with God so that our body, our life can be a place of worship. I am no better than you. I don't care how much longer I've been delivered. I read this book and my Bible over and over, and I spend time with God on a daily basis so that I can maintain my deliverance.

That's all you were missing: **maintenance**—your follow-up plan. Jesus, then, told this *former* adulterous woman how to maintain her deliverance. He said, "Follow Me."(v.12) God is not looking to condemn you of your sins, He's looking to forgive you for them. All you need to do is receive your forgiveness and then develop a relationship with God and maintain it by following Him. Reaffirm your commitment to serve Him. What are you waiting for? He's waiting on you . . .

"Return, O backsliding children," says the Lord; "for I am married to you." Jeremiah 3:14

Chapter Four: Breaking Free From The Identity Crisis

"God judges persons differently than humans do. Men and women look at the face; God looks into the heart." I Samuel 16:6-8 The Message

How many times have you said to yourself, "I'm going to get it right, really, I am. I'm going to stop doing all the stuff I'm doing that's not right. I'm going to stop smoking . . . I'm going to stop lying, stealing and cheating. I'm going to stop running the streets. I'm going to stop using drugs, really, I am. I'm really going to stop sleeping around and I'm going to stop having sex with any and everybody and then, I'm going to get my life right with God and then, I'll start going to church."

Well I've been there, done that before, too. Allow me to let you in on something: if you could get it right, you would have a long time ago. The clock is ticking and still, nothing has changed. You like to think that, with enough time, you'll get yourself together. Often, false impressions are given by satan, the world, and even from some church folks that you have to get it right before you come to Jesus. I find it mind blowing, simply amazing, that while I was IN my mess, all I had to do was accept Jesus. He didn't have to think about it, He didn't have to prepare Himself, nobody had to convince Him . . . The Lord was **ready** to forgive and save me, just like He said He would in Psalms 86:5.

"You mean to tell me that all I have to do is accept Jesus? Let me get this right . . . I don't have to join your church, I don't have to sing in the choir or work on the usher board? And I don't have to "catch" the Holy Ghost first or speak in tongues? Wait a minute now, I still do some stuff that I can't even tell my best friend and I still curse. Are you sure? Wait! Before you speak . .

. I still sleep around and I just left another lover last night . . . You sure?"

Oftentimes, we feel, or have felt, that we had to get it right first, clean up our mess or bribe God into saving us because we think salvation is too good to be true. In this world, you don't get something for nothing; so there's gotta be something else to it. But, thank Jesus, God is nothing like man! I was always thinking that the Lord wanted to send me to hell for my mess . . . when Jesus had already taken my place there . . . *at no cost to me!* Jesus had paid the price and all I had to do was accept and confess with my mouth Jesus Christ as Lord and believe in my heart that God has raised Him from the dead, simply as the Bible states in Romans 10:9.

That blows my left mind and it ought to blow yours, too! Look at your life . . . on your way straight to a forever hell, then Jesus, who knew no sin, takes your sin and your arrangements in hot hell, leaves it there, then comes with outstretched hands for you—just as you are?! My God, my God, you ought to stop reading right there, and thank Jesus. Every mistake you've made, even the ones only you and God know about . . . He loved you in spite of it! Psalms 103:8-12 declares, every sin committed . . . now REMOVED . . . blotted out!

> The LORD is merciful and gracious, slow to anger, and plenteous in mercy. He will not always chide: neither will he keep his anger for ever. He hath not dealt with us after our sins; nor rewarded us according to our iniquities. For as the heaven is high above the earth, so great is his mercy toward them that fear him. As far as the east is from the west, so far hath he removed our transgressions from us.

There's nothing worse than living your life on earth for satan and then spending eternity in hell with him. The penalty for sin is death. The only way you could have paid to get outta your mess was through death. And Jesus paid it for you. You ought to thank Jesus again for redeeming you, saving your soul and loving you—just as you are.

Now, I have to let you in on something: **the invitation to come as you are doesn't mean to stay as you are**. Jesus would not leave you in the state you came in. In fact, it would be an injustice for Him to leave you that way. What way? In church, with the title "saved" on your forehead, but on your way to meet your sex partner. Jumpin' and shoutin' while you're in the choir stand, but carrying condoms. You're seeing three women, my brother, and one of them is pregnant. Or you're seeing a fine man, sister, and he's married. Yeah, that way. Some of you are probably like I was. I wanted to be saved from hell, but not saved from my sins. My Bishop calls it fire insurance. All I knew was that I didn't want to go to hell. Unh, unh, hell's too hot and too long. It's forever and I felt the best thing for me to do was get my place secured in Heaven.

I was not interested in giving up sex and I certainly was not going to wait until I got married. But accepting Jesus as your Savior is not just about you getting to Heaven. If that's the case, you would have left here the moment you received Jesus. The Lord desires for you to live a victorious life in Him while you are here on earth and you can't live that kind of life staying as you are—in bondage to sexual sin. Let's go into this a littler deeper.

Some of us want to be saved as long as there's no pressure. We serve God only if it's convenient. In fact, in this time and age, many people claim they're saved, but the moment it's time to see the evidence of their salvation, they take off the title "Christian". There's no evidence at all that Jesus lives on the <u>inside</u> of you. We only want to live out the Word when either we need a blessing from God or when everything's "honky dory." Then we have that external appearance of being saved. The keyword here is "appearance." You wear the title of a Christian, but your lifestyle has not changed. We know the order of church so we say the right things, shout at the right time, and memorize a few Scriptures to quote, to fit into our "church conversations," but all the while, we continue to have active sex lives. This is what the Bible refers to as a form of godliness in II Timothy 3:1-5.

"This know also, that in the last days perilous times shall come. For men shall be lovers of their own selves, covetous, boasters, proud, blasphemers, disobedient to parents, unthankful, unholy, Without natural affection, trucebreakers, false accusers, incontinent, fierce, despisers of those that are good, Traitors, heady, high-minded, lovers of pleasures more than lovers of God; Having a form of godliness, but denying the power thereof: from such turn away.

Don't be naïve. There are difficult times ahead. As the end approaches, people are going to be self-absorbed, money-hungry, self-promoting, stuck-up, profane, contemptuous of parents, crude, coarse, dog-eat-dog, unbending, slanderers, impulsively wild, savage, cynical, treacherous, ruthless, bloated windbags, addicted to lust, and allergic to God. They'll make a show of religion, but behind the scenes they're animals. Stay clear of these people. (The Message Translation)

    Webster's dictionary defines the word "form" as a particular condition, character, or mode in which something appears; the manner or style of arranging and coordinating parts for a pleasing result. One particular definition of the word "form" that I found to be eyebrow raising stated that form can be "a document filled with blank spaces." The reason that I found this interesting is because it describes many of the single Christians who email me for advice or prayer. Let's take a look at an email recently sent to me.

> "I am from Uganda in East Africa and I am saved now 6 yrs but I have been in sexual sin as long as I can remember. I try to stop and go a couple of months without having sex but within no time I am in the same sin again and again. Yet, I go to church, I pray as normal Christians and even do what I need to do to look pure though I am

not in the eyes of God. My life was so bad and that's why I got saved but I am still living the same life of sex and sin. Is there anything I have not done yet? Ty Adams, I need prayer from you, I need to serve God, to live a pure life, not just say words which are true but then live a lie about everything else. Pray for me and tell me how I should go about this to overcome that burden. Thank you, you are the only one I have opened up to. I hope my life will change." S.K. in Africa (see response in our Q & A section on the website)

I believe that one of the reasons why we still find single Christians who have active sex lives is that they have not surrendered their sexual struggles to God. When you do not give the Lord access in the areas where you struggle, you walk around empty, giving space for ungodliness, without natural affection (homosexuality), lacking control of sexual gratification, masturbation, being addicted to lust, filling the spaces with fornication—relationship after relationship, from bed to bed, living impulsively wild lifestyles, and having allergic reactions to God. Now, we start running back and forth to the altar every other Sunday, but leave church the same way. The altar is the first step, but it does not save or deliver you; Jesus does. This is where we make the mistake. There's something else that has to take place: you have to surrender. When you are in sexual sin you lose your identity, the essence of who you are, and in order for you to break free and reclaim who you are in Christ, you have to surrender. Some of you have not surrendered this area of sexual sin to the Lord because we either don't believe that He can do it or you won't admit or acknowledge that you have a problem with sexual sin. First, let's deal with the fact of you even questioning God's ability to deliver you. My God, Who was and IS, before the beginning of time, Who created the heavens and the earth, Who is omniscient and knows all things, Who created you in your mother's womb, my God, Who is supreme in power, rank and authority, can do anything!

> ". . . understand that I am He. Before Me there was no God formed, nor shall there be after Me. I, even I, am the Lord, and besides Me there is no savior." Isaiah 43:10, 11

Matter of fact, you need God. He is the only one who can save and deliver you. The Bible says, in Matthew 19:26, that with God ALL things are possible.[6] God is not bound by anything! So, the question is not, "Can He do it?" The question is, "Do you want to be delivered?!" Let me set the record straight. satan didn't create sex; he distorted it. God created sex; He's the mastermind behind it and it was created for two people who have entered into a covenant of marriage ONLY. With that said, if He created it for covenant, by all means, wouldn't He have created a means of keeping you until you say, "I do"?

> Now unto Him that is able to keep you from falling, and to present you faultless before the presence of His glory with exceeding joy. Jude 24

He has a means of keeping you. Not only is it His desire and His will for you to be set free, but it is also His desire to have fellowship with you. The only way to bring yourself into His presence is to remove the fault and the sin. Sexual sin places a wall between you and God and it paralyzes you. Its grip cripples you and causes you to be ineffective. Imagine a humid, hot, 98-degree summer day with no air conditioner. You ask someone to bring you an ice-cold glass of water but they bring it to you in a dirty glass. It's useless. God cannot use a dirty vessel. There's no question about it, Jesus wants to present you faultless before God.

Let's look at the acknowledging aspect of it. Some of us are guilty of looking at sin in degrees or levels. As if one has greater weight than the other. IF YOU HAVE ANY SEX OUTSIDE OF MARRIAGE, IT IS SIN. Let me clarify again what I mean by "any." Fornication is not just having sexual intercourse with someone you are not married to. From homosexuality to masturbation to pornography to oral sex—it's all sexual sin. You are going to have to be open and honest about where you are at for you to be set free. In fact, confession has to take place for your salvation. Confessing your fault to the Lord does not make you less of a man or a woman.

This openness on your part allows and gives Him access and permission to deliver and set you free from this area that has entangled you for far too long. He's not going to go there if you don't let Him. This means we have to expose some areas in your life in order for change to take place. To expose means to subject a sensitive area to the action of light. Exposing the sensitive area may be a little uncomfortable, but if you allow yourself to become subject to Jesus, the Light, you will no longer be bound—bound by any darkness that satan has tried to consume your life with. You can and **WILL** overcome sexual sin!

Another reason why we don't surrender is because we don't want to go through the changes needed to be delivered and set free. There are some changes that you must go through and we don't want to because it's work (especially for those of us who have served God out of convenience). **After your conversion, there's a process of sanctification**. It's sort of like road construction. I'll admit, I do NOT like road construction, but I don't like potholes either. Try driving in one. The Department of Public Works will often do some temporary stuff, like filling in the potholes first, but that only works for a minute. Eventually, they're going to have to close down the road and repave.

This means road barriers, longer commutes, sitting still because nothing or nobody's moving, detours—total inconvenience! But God has to lay a new foundation in you and the ground has to be broken first. All that old stuff that's been hindering you from being delivered and set free has to come out of you. Your old way of thinking has to go! Your old way of doing things has to go!

> And that means killing off everything connected with that way of death: sexual promiscuity, impurity, lust, doing whatever you feel like whenever you feel like it, and

grabbing whatever attracts your fancy. That's a life shaped by things and feelings instead of by God. Colossians 3:5 The Message

You can't go where God is about to take you with that in you, and patching it up, covering it up, and avoiding it is not an option. It only delays it, because eventually, the old you, the old way of doing things, will only come back and destroy you. It's like driving on black ice. Black ice is tricky; it's a sheet of ice that's on the road but you can't see it. That's just how sin is: white sin. You're driving on the road of sin, thinking everything's cool because you've been doing this for a while and have suffered no consequences (yet). Don't allow satan to fool you. There's nothing black about ice; surely, there's nothing white or pure about sin.

The Bible clearly states the wages of sin is death (Romans 6:23). The reason satan lures you into his trap, makes you think that serving God is going to be boring, no fun, and submitting to the Word of God is going to be hard and difficult so that he can have authority over your life. 1 John 5:3 says that His commandments are not a burden or are difficult to do. God will equip you and empower you to do what honors Him most. I'm here to expose that liar satan, so you can be delivered and set free. You no longer have to be bound and be held captive to him.

A lot of people do not like this part of the process because it is not easy. You have to give up things and people who have been a part of your life that have been trespassing. But this is not an option: you have to surrender to Jesus. Folks might "hate on you" because you can't hang out with them anymore, and they'll be mad because they can't put their hands and their mouth on you like they used to. You will be talked about, and probably considered "holier than thou," but I guarantee you that it will be more than worth it. The best part about it is that you will come out of the refining fire with no trace of smoke on you; God will fireproof you and He will never leave you . . . He'll be with you through the entire process as promised in Isaiah 43:1, 2.

> "BUT NOW [in spite of past judgments for Israel's sins], thus says the Lord, He Who created you, O Jacob, and He Who formed you, O Israel: Fear not, for I have redeemed you [ransomed you by paying a price instead of leaving you captives]; I have called you by your name; you are Mine. ²When you pass through the waters, I will be with you, and through the rivers, they will not overwhelm you. When you walk through the fire, you will not be burned or scorched, nor will the flame kindle upon you."

All the Biblical principles, information, steps of deliverance, and revelation in this book means nothing if you do not put it to action. It means nothing to have faith, and know what to do, but you will not "do" or put into action what you know. James 2:20 emphatically states that "It's just dead knowledge." The first thing we note here in 1 Peter 1:13-15 is that you must begin preparing your mind for action.

> Therefore, prepare your minds for action; be self-controlled; set your hope fully on the grace to be given you when Jesus Christ is revealed. As obedient children, do not conform to the evil desires you had when you lived in ignorance. But just as He who called you is holy, so be holy in all you do; for it is written: "Be holy, because I am holy. I Peter 1:13-16 NIV

Another thing to note is that you are in ignorance when you conform to the worldly acts and evil desires of people who do not live for Jesus. You ignored the truth; that's where ignorance comes from: a deliberate neglect or disregard of God. It's important, now more than ever, to regard or esteem the Word of God highly and consistently. You cannot afford to be a part-time Christian because the adversary, satan, is waiting for just that opportunity. He is always on the clock.

Your Bible, your manual, needs to be a working document in your life daily and you need to apply the Word to every situation in your life. In order for you not to conform to ignorance again, you have to transform your mind by renewing it continually. Let's look at Romans 12 again. In paraphrasing it, the apostle Paul pleads with us to offer ourselves as a living sacrifice. The sacrifice that we just talked about is for life—it is represented daily. You deal with the world daily. Remember, that residue has to be burned off daily. Offer your bodies to a life of surrendering, a life that is holy and acceptable to God which is your reasonable service . . . Stop right there. <u>Your body is to be presented holy</u>. One of my favorite quotes from my spiritual father, Dr. Myles Munroe is "God doesn't want us to develop holiness, because He never intended that we would not be holy".

Holy: declared sacred and pure; consecrated
Sacred: secured by reverence against violation
Consecrated: to devote to some purpose; set apart

You are holy. That was not a misprint; **you are holy.** The problem is that you've always been told that you wear filthy rags and just a sinner saved by grace. This is one reason why we have so many single folks sleeping around; they don't know who they are. Whenever I buy my niece, Promise, some new gym shoes, she will do anything she can to avoid getting them dirty. It can be the slightest drip, or a drop of rain outside, and she will not wear them. "I don't want to step in any mud with my gear on." You are not filthy rags, you've been washed and purified by the Blood of Jesus! When God created you, He created you in His image: HOLY. He has declared you sacred and pure and that's how He sees you, holy. The dilemma is you have not caught up with the person God created you to be.

The world has conformed and altered your original state and now your mind has to be transformed and renewed to the holiness that God created you in. When you know that you have been declared holy, you will not allow anything to tamper with that. Some fool can step on you and it will annoy and anger you. They would even try to get you to have sex with them. Like my niece, Promise, you will refuse to get into anything that will get you dirty. You have to refuse to go back and lie in dirt, and you have to avoid anything that will contaminate you **at all costs.** Besides, it's only a cheap thrill . . . Take a couple doses of "Salt Peter" every day. Don't consider what it will cost you . . . **Consider what it's worth.**

"Throw out anything tainted with evil. May God himself, the God who makes everything holy and whole, and make you holy and whole, put you together-spirit, soul, and body-and keep you fit for the coming of our Master, Jesus Christ. The One who called you is completely dependable. If he said it, he'll do it!" I Thessalonians 5:22-25 The Message

Allow God to do it. Surrender. If you don't master sexual sin, it will master you. You've been fighting and toiling with this same issue—wrestling with your flesh. You've been struggling even in your mind, falling repeatedly back in sexual sin, and you've been told that you can't overcome this, that you can't do it . . . You're right, you can't do it . . . Jesus can. You can't do this without Him . . . Surrender. We can't go on to the next chapter of this book or the next chapter of your life, until you surrender. You are not the only one with this struggle. Thousands of other people who are even reading this book right now, who want to be delivered, have to go through the same route. You are not the only one. I know that satan will make you think that you are the only one in the church struggling with sexual sin, but don't you believe it for one minute!

Before I surrendered to Jesus I was present in the church faithfully, tithing, attending mid-week Bible study and conferences, praying in tongues, quoting Scriptures in my sleep—but still in bondage to sexual sin. I said, "Lord, I'll do whatever You want, but don't talk or deal with me about sex. You can talk to me about whatever You want. Do You want me to get on the usher board or volunteer some of my time? Whatever You want, but don't talk to me about sexual sin."

That area was off-limits and until I allowed God in this area, I stayed in somebody else's bed. But I decided that I no longer wanted to live my life outside of His will and I wanted to be made whole in every area of my life. Now, I am no longer bound, but I've been set free and I say to you, if you truly desire to be delivered—and you do, otherwise, you wouldn't have picked up this book. I don't care if it's your first time or your "fifty-if" time down this road. I don't care how long you've been away and I don't care if you are a backslider, just slide back. It's just that simple . . . Take the first step: SURRENDER. Know that He has accepted you just the way you are-sin and all.

Put yourself under arrest. Come out, come out with your hands up, your hands lifted up to Him and surrender. You have the right to remain silent, anything you say can and will be counted against you. You have a choice; God gives you a choice to stay in your dead sin life or be delivered. You can let it count against you by continuing to operate under the law of sin and death and allow the things you've been doing, and send you to hell, OR, you can give up that right and you can be set free from it by the law of the Spirit of Life in Christ Jesus (Romans 8:2).[11] You have a right to an attorney, if you can't afford one, Jesus has already paid the cost for you and one will be appointed for you. He will wipe that sin record of yours clean. Every filthy, dirty sin you've committed, instantly off your record, wiped away! You can stand before God, the Supreme Judge, with an acquittal . . . all charges dropped! Now that you've been read your rights, would you like to make this statement with me:

Lord Jesus, I come to You with my hands lifted up, surrendering. I can't stay as I am. I've shielded you out and have gone against Your will and Your Word. I have fought too long with sexual sin and I no longer will allow the devil to have authority and control over my life. Satan, I cancel every attack and every assignment you thought you had on my life and I am no longer in bondage to you or to sexual sin. I take the handcuffs off of me and place them on you; I am no longer bound! The Bible says in 1 John 1:9 that if I confess my sins, that You, Lord would be faithful and just to forgive my sins and You would cleanse me from all unrighteousness.

I repent and turn away from sin, sins that I recognize and even the ones that I am not aware of. Shape and mold me like only You can. Remove anything that's not like You. Create in me a clean heart, Lord, and renew in me a right spirit. My desire is to please You. Enlighten my eyes to a greater understanding of You and Your Word. Open my eyes to see as You see. I thank You for loving me with an everlasting love, for forgiving me, blotting out my sins, cleansing me and placing me back in right standing with You. I thank You, Lord, for accepting me as I am, but, most of all, for not leaving me that way. You are Lord over my life and I give You complete access to every area of my life to bring about the change You desire to see. I thank you for what You've done and for what You're about to do in my life and I claim it, in the Mighty Name of Jesus. AMEN.

Praise the name of the Lord, you've been set free from the hands of the enemy! You are no longer bound and you have the victory! You've just made a powerful stand by surrendering. Be confident and assured of this very thing: that He which hath begun a good work in you will perform (complete) it until day of Jesus Christ (Philippians 1:6). With the access you've just given the Lord, the chapters ahead will show you how you can allow Him to complete the work in you and how to never become captive to the devil in this area of your life ever again.

Chapter Five: Reclaiming Your Body

"Have compassion on me, LORD, for I am weak. Heal me, LORD, for my body is in agony." Psalms 6:2 (NLT)

All too often many Christians are associated and attached to their old life after they have received salvation. This primarily happens because people often say, "It's my body and I can do what I want to do with it." But let's look at what the Manufacturer, who created you and sex, has to say about it.

"Now, the body is not for sexual immorality but for the Lord, and the Lord for the body. And God both raised up the Lord and will also raise us up by His power. Do you not know that your bodies are members of Christ? Shall I then take the members of Christ and make them members of a harlot? Certainly not! Or do you not know that he who is joined to a harlot is one body with her? For "the two," He says, "shall become one flesh." But he who is joined to the Lord is one spirit with Him. Flee sexual immorality. Every sin that a man does is outside the body, but he who commits sexual immorality sins against his own body. Or do you not know that your body is the temple of the Holy Spirit who is in you, whom you have from God, and you are not your own? For you were bought at a price; therefore, glorify God in your body and in your spirit, which are God's." I Corinthians 6:13-20

Since you have accepted Jesus as your Lord and Savior, you have forfeited satan's rights and ownership and gave yourself, including your body, over to the Lord. When you accepted Jesus, you acknowledged the fact that the Master honored you with His body and He took your place in hell for the sins that you have committed when you proclaimed Him as Lord over your life. He immediately took up residence on the inside of you.

Now, if satan was still your lord, then it would be quite okay to have sex outside of marriage and you could do whatever you wanted to do with your body. But that's not the case. Jesus is Lord.

> "Don't you realize that whatever you choose to obey becomes your master? You can choose sin, which leads to death, or you can choose to obey God and receive his approval." Romans 6:16 (NLT)

Whoever is lord is the owner of the property and makes the guidelines and rules of the property. Since Jesus is Lord over you, then He makes the guidelines and the rules. This means you can't do whatever you want to do.

> Don't you see that you can't live however you please, squandering what God paid such a high price for? (The Message)

It surprises me when people put a high value on the church (and you should), but the y don't put a high value on their body. After everyone has left church and gone home, would you sprawl between the pews and have sex? The thought of it is repulsive! Then why would you let someone go inside you, the temple, and have sex? *Or didn't you realize that your body is a sacred place, the place of the Holy Spirit?* God places a greater value on you than He does the church because He lives inside of you. The Lord also gave us guidelines for having sex in I Corinthians 7:1-2 (NLT):

"First, is it a good thing to have sexual relations? Certainly, but only within a certain context. It's good for a man to have a wife and for a woman to have a husband. Sexual drives are strong, but marriage is strong enough to contain them and provide for a balanced and fulfilling sexual life in a world of sexual disorder."

The first thing worth noting is that it is good for a man to have a <u>wife</u>-not a playmate, a girl-toy, a main squeeze or any other part-time lover, but a <u>wife</u>. And it is good for a woman to have a <u>husband</u>, not a suga' daddy, not a weekend lover, nor a boyfriend who provides sexual pleasures, but a <u>husband</u>. Sex used in any other way outside of the guidelines of this Scripture is considered sexual immorality. There are no in-betweens, ifs, ands, or buts about it; no alterations can be made. Sex was created by God to be enjoyed within the context of marriage of a man and a woman, period. It was created for procreation, pleasure, for the means of expressing your love for your husband/wife, and to seal the covenant that you have.

The problem is, we want the blessings (sex) that God gives but we don't want to operate in the plan of God (marriage). We want sex without the commitment, but God's plan does not work that way. If you do not do it God's way, there are severe consequences. You need to understand that sex is very powerful; the drive of sex is strong and potent. So, just as you wouldn't climb up on a pole and mess with the power lines to turn your lights on, you shouldn't climb up in someone else's bed to get turned on. You're messing with high voltage! What you end up doing is misusing or abusing, distorting, and corrupting the very essence of sex when you do not operate in its original intent: marriage. And more importantly, understand this: sexual sin becomes addictive. An addiction to sex forms when you try to use sex to satisfy or improve fulfillment through inordinate means. And like a drug, the hook is not just physical.

> "Here's how a prostitute operates. She has sex with her clients, takes a bath, then asks who's next." Proverbs 30:20 (The Message)

I continued to have sex after I got saved, I didn't change my lifestyle. I switched locations and became a "temple prostitute"- a **prostitute in the church.** I found myself lying with someone all week long, going to midweek Bible study, paying my tithes, going to church on Sunday morning and "take a bath," but then I went to have sex again. The hook of sin will have you numb to the Word and everything else. You'll go to church and the pastor will even talk about the consequences of sexual sin and provide a means for redemption, but you'll go right back out and have sex with someone you are not married to. Then with no conscience whatsoever, you will turn around and show up on Sunday morning smelling like midnight sex with a dab of perfume on, thinking you've covered it up and no one knows what you did the night before. Think again. You only fool yourself.

When a man and a woman make a marital vow before the Lord they share a covenant with one another. The husband and the wife literally become one during the sexual union, thereby sealing their covenant, and sex is used as the seal on the marriage by the Holy Spirit. **But sexual intercourse seals a man and a woman regardless if they are married or not.** In other words, when you have sex outside of marriage, contrary to God's way, an **unholy spirit SEALS** you and that man or woman. You allow satan to become lord over you when you operate under his guidelines of sexual immorality/sin. If you submit to sin, then you give him permission to seal you with an unholy spirit. You become one or join yourself to that person whether you are married to them or not. So, whatever they are, you are. Whatever sexually transmitted diseases (STDs) they might have, you will have. AIDS, syphilis, gonorrhea, herpes, whatever they've picked up along the way from other sex partners they have had, they can give to you. Whatever you join yourself with, you become one with as stated in I Corinthians 6:16. And that's not just sexually transmitted diseases or infections, but **SPIRITUALLY** transmitted diseases, as well.

> "There's more to sex than mere skin on skin. Sex is as much a spiritual mystery as a physical fact. As written in Scripture, "The two become one." I Corinthians 6:16 (The Message)

Infection is defined as contaminated by disease, to affect with disease, or affect so as to influence **feeling** or **action.** Spirits are transferred during sexual intercourse and whatever spirits your partner has, you have (lust, manic or physical depression, demonic or lying spirits, evil desires, filthiness of flesh, deception, instability, lack of commitment, lasciviousness, etc. Understand that the infected spirit of the person you have sex with influences how you feel and act because of the transferring of their spirit to you. The Bible says in Genesis 4:1 that Adam **knew** Eve when he had sex with her. That's what sexual intimacy does; it gives you full knowledge, <u>inside</u> information, about the person you are sleeping with and you become what you know. In other words, **what we intimately do with our bodies affects the spiritual states of our soul.** If you had sex outside of marriage then you've been infected; whoever you slept with contaminated you. No wonder you keep hopping from bed to bed—flesh outta control, addicted to pornography, several bed partners, wild orgies, desires for someone of the same sex, having affairs with a married man. You've been sleeping with the enemy. A single man or woman is one spirit with the Lord, therefore, when you have engaged in sexual intercourse, you sever your union with the Lord. When you lie with a harlot, you become a harlot. And God is not-and will never be a harlot.

> "Do you not know that your bodies are members of Christ? Shall I then take the members of Christ and make them members of a harlot? Certainly not! Or do you not know that he who is joined to a harlot is one body with her? For "the two," He says, "shall become one flesh." I Corinthians 6:15-17

One of the main reasons why satan wants you to have sex outside of marriage is because he knows that it will separate or divide you from the Lord. This is why the Bible says "flee", run from sexual immorality. When you operate under the realm of sexual immorality, satan infects you with a demonic, spiritually transmitted disease. And *this* disease will cause sickness, disease, nguish, torment, confusion, despair, shame, guilt, , perversions, addictions, spiritual, physical and eternal

You've even experienced that death before. It's that death feeling that comes over you. That emptiness you feel after the stars have left your head and the two minutes of pleasure have ended. The teardrops that run down your face hit the pillow you lie on. That feeling of hopelessness, defeat, shame and guilt as you try to swallow the lump in your throat; angered, because your panties and your self-respect are on the floor. You try to play it off to your bed partner as if nothing's wrong. Or maybe you couldn't play it off; you couldn't hold it until you got into the hotel lobby or into your car. Instead, you broke right there. Right in front of the man you just had sex with.

I know the feeling. It's one of the worst feelings you could ever experience—like a child hiding under the bed because you've crushed your father's heart. You can't believe you even did it-after you said you wouldn't again. The last time was supposed to have been the last time. Yet, you did it again. Some of you sincerely meant that you wouldn't do it again, but because of the contamination, you fell prey to the enemy . . . again. You thought you wouldn't fall because you said, "I'm not going to give in to temptation." But what happened? The contamination of sexual sin left you so blind and unstable that you can't recognize when you were in trouble. You thought you were under control but you really weren't. It's impossible to get back up from the bed of sin, go back to "normal", and then be able to withstand temptation the next time it calls. Contamination has reduced your ability and power to withstand, and those infectious spirits that were attached to you begin to rear their ugly heads.

I had a friend named Monica, single and in her twenties, who I considered to be a "down to earth" Christian, an "about her Father's business" type of girl, started hanging around some family members who were the drinking, sleeping around, hanging out, partyin'-all-night type. At first, she appeared to be cool, ministering and witnessing to them but eventually she started "innocently" hanging out with them. She met this guy who "somewhat" believed in the Lord (you know, the dangerous type). In a short period of time, she had sex with him. It didn't work out.

Then, shortly after that, she moved on and met someone else, slept with him, and before she knew it, "fell" into sexual sin with four men over a six-month period of time. We use that term "fell" too loosely. She didn't fall. What happens is that the space of time between bed partners closes and tightens because the effects of sexual sin is set up to be that way; before you know it, you are out of control. Sexual sin does not stop until it destroys or kills you.

> "Lust gets pregnant, and has a baby: sin! Sin grows up to adulthood, and becomes a real killer." James 1:15 (The Message)

Sex outside of marriage is **never** free; it will cost you so much, and the thief, satan, is coming to collect. A crime has been committed. Let's go to the scene of the crime: your body. There are 6.7 billion people on earth and no one is like you. You are one of a kind, even if you are a twin. Your fingerprint identifies who you are and no one else has your fingerprint. If you were dusted for fingerprints, how many would we find on you? Have you allowed so many fingerprints on you that your identity has been smeared and you don't know who you are because so many other people have left their life on you? Besides the fingerprints and residue from all the bed partners you've had, there are scars on your mind, cuts and the wounds are on your heart, because the consequences of sexual sin are tormenting.

> "It is obvious what kind of life develops out of trying to get your own way all the time: repetitive, loveless, cheap sex; a stinking accumulation of mental and emotional garbage; frenzied and joyless grabs for happiness; trinket gods; magic-show religion; paranoid loneliness; cutthroat competition; all-

consuming-yet-never-satisfied wants; a brutal temper; an impotence to love or be loved; divided homes and divided lives; small-minded and lopsided pursuits; the vicious habit of depersonalizing everyone into a rival; uncontrolled and uncontrollable addictions; ugly parodies of community. I could go on. This isn't the first time I have warned you, you know. If you use your freedom this way, you will not inherit God's Kingdom." Galatians 5:19–21 (The Message)

As this scripture passage shows us, the cost of sin is insurmountable! Much of the drama, stress, and turmoil in your life is due to the compromise you've made through sexual pleasures obtained illegally. And if that's not enough, to spend eternity in hell for them is more than you bargain for. To go back to sexual sin is simply not worth it. The Bible says in 1 Corinthians 15:52 that Jesus is coming back in the twinkling of an eye, quicker than you can blink. You can't afford to be caught in a 6-second orgasm with your pants or your panties down. Once you've reclaimed your body to the Lord and begin to treat is as God intended, you can be delivered of the torment, become shackle-proof and never get into bondage with sexual sin again!

    Many of you have been trying to solve a spiritual need, a spiritual problem, with a physical or profane solution. You need spiritual healing, not sexual healing. You've been trying to use sex as a substitute for intimacy. But "making love" does not make him or her "love" you. Attempting to use relationships and sex to complete you will not work. Sex will not drive loneliness away or fulfill you. It will only tear you apart and loneliness will become emptiness. Instead of fulfilling a void, your sexual exploits will create one. Trying to escape by running into a relationship will not cause you to live and grow, but instead it will eventually surface as death attached to a life support because you become dependent on a man/woman to breathe.

    "Hi, Ty, my name is Sharese and I watched the 700 club one night and I saw you on there. I'm struggling. I am in a relationship now for three months and my boyfriend already wants to have sex with me and I am afraid if I say no he will break up with me. I am a Christian and I have been saved and I know this is not the right path for me, but I don't want to be alone. Please help me. I don't want to end up in a situation that is not good for me."

Many of you have been looking in the wrong places, plugging yourself up to the wrong people. A brother with his lips on your hips or someone's hands in your panties, ladies, is **not** the answer. Having sex with someone will not fulfill your ultimate need. Your quest for fulfillment continues because you have been searching for a climax that you will never find in a man or a woman. You can only get life and real intimacy from the Source and because you have yet to develop an up-and-close, personal relationship with God, you continue to run on empty— in search of something you could never find because you were searching for it in the wrong people who could never fill the void. God is the only One who can fulfill it . . . let Him. Let Him become your life support. Allow Him to finally end the repeated cycle of dependent relationships.

"Jesus replied, "People soon become thirsty again after drinking this water. But the water I give them takes away thirst altogether. It becomes a perpetual spring within them, giving them eternal life."

"Please, sir," the woman said, "give me some of that water! Then I'll never be thirsty again, and I won't have to come here to haul water."

"Go and get your husband," Jesus told her.
"I don't have a husband," the woman replied.
Jesus said, "You're right! You don't have a husband--for you have had five husbands, and you aren't even married to the man you're living with now." John 4:13-18

Jesus introduces the Living Water to this thirsty Samaritan woman and her response was, "Please, give me some of that water!" She knew she needed Jesus. She said, "I'll never thirst again." This is a common mentality of many Christians: "as long as I get to Jesus." Yes, that's true, but look at Jesus' response, "Where is your man?" She was ready to get the water, but Jesus asked her about the men in her life. Understand, Jesus can hook you up with the Water, but if you don't get rid of what's dehydrating you, you will continue to get thirsty. Thirsty means to have a physical condition resulting from an inner need and all too often that physical condition is a sexual relationship.

Getting a drink is not enough. Getting "saved" is not enough. You have to get rid of what's depleting you. Jesus told this woman that she had five other men, plus the one she was currently with, and that she had made them her husbands. Jesus knew she was not married to any one of them, but He called them her husbands. You bond and enter into a covenant with every person that you have sex with, as we discussed in the previous chapters. Jesus, in essence, was saying, "Now, I can quench or put an end to your thirst, I can satisfy you, but every time you take a sip of this water, the men, the drainpipes in your life will dehydrate you. You've had six sex partners and you are still thirsty. You have an inner need that a man or sex cannot fulfill."

Jesus knew exactly what He was talking about because He, too, had been in a thirsty state. He knew what it was like to be thirsty. In John 19:28 when He was on the Cross, He said, "I thirst." Anyone separated from God becomes thirsty. Jesus was separated from God on the cross because of our sins that were on Him. Every time you lay down with someone in sin, every time you allow yourself to get into these toxic relationships, it separates you from the Father and you become thirsty, again and again. You are going to come back to the well to haul for water until you leave your pot and get rid of the people in your life who are drainpipes. When this woman left her pot, she was saying, "I'm not going to need it, because I'm getting rid of what is draining me." You have to come to the place that you say, "Lord, I allow You to take away what's draining me."

The Lord made many things, but He created only one thing to have a personal relationship with Him: You. He's desired that the whole time; so has your soul. That's what your inner need is. That's what you have been looking for all this time-a personal, intimate relationship with God. As you begin to take on who you are in Christ, the Lord begins to recover everything you lost while you were in your sexual traps. Your intimate relationship with the Father begins to reclaim parts of you that were stolen so that you can become whole again. You are not alone, He is with you.

> "If you'll hold on to me for dear life," says God, "I'll get you out of any trouble. I'll give you the best of care if you'll only get to know and trust me. Call me and I'll answer, be at your side in bad times; I'll rescue you."
> Psalms 91:14–15 (The Message)

Chapter 6: Reclaiming Your Mind

"Examine me, GOD, from head to foot, order your battery of tests. Make sure I'm fit inside and out so I never lose sight of your love, but keep in step with you, never missing a beat." Psalms 26:2, 3 (The Message)

    I often get this one particular question from single Christians asking, "At what point did you *know* you were delivered from sexual sin?" This question is often posed because many people want to know how they can pinpoint if they have been delivered. Declaring Jesus as Lord, making a vow and stating that you are surrendering your life and your body to the Jesus is one thing, but to see the manifestation of that commitment is another. Like some of you, I didn't feel a thing. I didn't see anything magical happen before my eyes, nor did I feel a sudden rush or my body change in an instant. No zing, no zap, no nothing! Well, giving your life to Jesus is not about a feeling. The misconception is that you have to "feel saved." The problem is we have always been moved by our emotions, by what feels good. Stars have to circle around your head, a chill has to go down your spine and then you fall down on the floor, spin around, and hit your head on the pew. That's what I love about Jesus, the requirement to accept Him as our Savior is not complicated at all. The proof is simply in the pudding. You know that you are saved from a burning hell, not by what you feel, but you determine it by 1 John 3:4–10:

> All who indulge in a sinful life are dangerously lawless, for sin is a major disruption of God's order. Surely you know that Christ showed up in order to get rid of sin. There is no sin in Him, and sin is not part of His program.

No one who lives deeply in Christ makes a practice of sin
. . . It's the person who acts right who is right, just as we
see it lived out in our righteous Messiah. Those who make
a practice of sin are straight from the devil, the pioneer in
the practice of sin. The Son of God entered the scene to
abolish the devil's ways.

People conceived and brought into life by God don't
make a practice of sin . . . It's not in the nature of the
God-begotten to practice and parade (walk up and down
in) sin. Here's how you tell the difference between God's
children and the devil's children: The one who won't
practice righteous ways isn't from God . . . a simple test."
(The Message)

It's just that simple. You know that you have been set free from the devil because you do not practice sin, but you practice righteous ways. Practiced sin is a repeated habit. You've repeated it so much that it's regular behavior for you; you begin to unconsciously repeat it where it almost becomes involuntary. Some of you thought that you would automatically stop sinning once you gave your life to Jesus. No, your body still desires to go and lie down and have some sex. Then, when you had sex with someone again, you question whether you were saved or not. You begin to doubt the whole "saved" scene. This is why some of you left the church. Your struggle with sexual sin made you believe that Jesus never saved you in the first place.

Let me put it this way: if you have sex with someone on Monday night, are you still saved? You repent, ask God for forgiveness, you're "resaved" now. But then, on Tuesday afternoon, you slept with someone again. Did you lose your salvation? Your deeds and good works did not get you any merits with Jesus and neither did your good morals credit anything to your salvation; it was only God's grace that pulled you from the jaws of hell. Hence, your good girl/good boy behavior does not sustain or renew your membership in God's family.

"So what do we do? Keep on sinning so God can keep on forgiving? I should hope not! If we've left the country where sin is sovereign, how can we still live in our old house there? Or didn't you realize we packed up and left there for good?" Romans 6:1-3 (The Message)

To continuously live as single, saved, and having sex is not an option! Neither is using 1 John 1:9 as a get-out-of-sin free card. The first thing you do is realize that you have left the country, the life of sin, and you have a new residence. The question was posed, "How can you?" The answer is, "You can't." You can no longer allow sin to have reign over you or to have rank in your life. That's like getting married, but never leaving the place you stayed in to move in with your husband or wife. That would be crazy! That's exactly what took place when you gave satan his walking papers. You told sin, "It's over!" So, it would be foolish to still live or even spend the weekend over sin's house when you now live at salvation's house.

Another question was posed in the scripture we just read: "Didn't you realize that we packed up and left there for good?" This implies that if you are a person who is now saved, but still camps out with sin, you could possibly not realize that you have relocated. "Oops, I forgot I was saved!" That may sound pretty amusing to some of you, but I once heard someone say that the flesh that some of you live in, does not even know that you are saved. Your flesh is like, "Hold on a minute, we were doing just fine until you packed up and moved. I was comfortable where we were living. But that doesn't matter, we can just take what we had in our old house and move it into the new one."

The Apostle Paul said you have to realize, grasp and understand clearly that you packed up and left for good. This, now, has to become your reality. You now live your life strictly for Jesus. Your mind has to catch up with who you are. The question is, "Who are you, really?" Let's look at what took place when you gave Jesus your life. When you denounced satan and repented your sins, you accepted Jesus as your Savior, then, He saved, redeemed and rescued you from hell. This is commonly known as salvation. This is where we get the word "salvage". Jesus saved your spirit man from the power and penalties of sin. Most people believe that salvation is just that: escapism from hell. Yes, it is that, but salvation is also healing, peace, wholeness, and deliverance. You were completely redeemed and restored! God came back to get what was His.

Here's another example. You go into the store and to buy some soda. You don't want the bottle; you just want the soda that's in it. Now, if you have a soda bottle that has a ten-cent deposit on it when you purchase it, you'll have to pay the cost for the soda and the deposit. After using the contents in the bottle, you can redeem or get back the ten-cent deposit you paid. This is Ty's parable for what took place. God wanted the contents inside the bottle: you. In order to get you, there was a cost: Jesus, plus a deposit—His Blood. The bottle (the sin you were in) was given back, but the deposit—the Blood of Jesus—was redeemed, and so were you. Now, that deposit that was used to redeem you contained the power and the ability to totally salvage you, giving you healing, peace, wholeness and deliverance. The issue is getting you to realize that you are no longer trapped inside that bottle of sin. You are now back to your original state, before sin. Your mind needs to catch up and realize that your spirit has been redeemed.

You are made of spirit, soul, and body. The life of a man is the spirit of man. When you accepted Jesus as your Savior, this is the realm where the born-again process took place, the realm that received eternal life. This is also the realm where you and God communicate because God is a Spirit and He responds to you through your spirit. Now, your soul is the mental arena where your will, desires, and emotions live in. This is the intellect of man, where you reason and think, where you have the capacity to sense or feel. Thirdly, your body or flesh is simply the arena where the spirit and mind are housed in. It is the physical part of you that functions because of the other two realms (spirit and soul).

The first thing you need to note is that only your spirit is born again, not your soul, nor your body. The only change that took place was in your spirit; it was the only realm that was renewed back to its original state. That original state is the image of God, as we read in Genesis 1:26:

Then God said, "Let us make people in our image, to be like ourselves. They will be masters over all life . . . So God created people in his own image; God patterned them after himself; male and female he created them.

You are made, fashioned, and patterned after God Himself! You have His character and His nature; you are just like your Father, a spitting image! What is God's character and nature like? I'm glad you asked. I Peter 1:16 says:

"Be holy; for I am holy."

Holy means to be consecrated, set apart, pure, and sanctified.

God is Holy. It is His nature or natural character to be holy. It is His existence. God breathes and holiness comes out of Him; it is His substance. Holiness is not what God does, but it is who He is. Now, put a mirror up to your face. **You are looking at God**. The Word just said that you are in the image of God and you have been patterned after Him. In fact, in Genesis 2, it says that when God formed man, He breathed into his nostrils the breath of life. God is life and the source of life. God breathed Himself into you. My God, my God . . . you are God's breath, walking and moving throughout the earth! So, if God is the source of life and the source of holiness, then, when He breathed into you, you not only inhaled life, but you inhaled holiness. If that's the case, hen you exhale, holiness comes out of you. I have a question, then . . . why are you still "waiting to exhale"? Why are you waiting to be holy? Just, exhale!

Oh, it's not that easy, huh? Why, when it's natural for you to be holy. Some of us have what I call "layaway mentality": pay on it a 'lil here, a 'lil there. "I'll use or exercise a little holiness and I'll get the rest out later. God knows I'm trying; He knows my faults . . . I'm not perfect… He understands when I slip." No,

God did not say try to live holy, He said **be** holy, because I created you in holiness. So be that. That layaway mentality will only get you in further mess, because sin begets sin.

You can't think that you can just go and sleep with this person "just one last time." No, sin wants more and more of it. It'll have you thinking, "I'm not perfect. I might as well." But, remember, sin begets sin. It'll have you doing far more than you bargained for. You'll start going to places you never even desired. If that one last time won't have you in wild orgies, it'll have you watching pornography. Then it'll take you to drinking and smoking, to lying and cheating. Sin wakes up other sins. Luke 11:24-26 tells us:

"When a corrupting spirit is expelled from someone, it drifts along through the desert looking for an oasis, some unsuspecting soul it can bedevil. When it doesn't find anyone, it says, "I'll go back to my old haunt." On return, it finds the person swept and dusted, but vacant. It then runs out and rounds up seven other spirits dirtier than itself and they all move in, whooping it up. That person ends up far worse than if he'd never gotten cleaned up in the first place." (The Message)

You can't afford to play with sin. The devil is not playing; John 10:10 tells us he's out for the kill. You can't think that you can live a life for Jesus and go back and dabble in sin and you'll be fine, that nothing will happen. No, you'll find yourself worse than you were before you got saved. The Scripture here said that it'll return and find you swept and dusted, but vacant, which means not occupied, or inhabited as a house; not filled or held as a job or a position, free from activity or care; empty.

You've been cleaned up by God, but empty. Where is your substance? Your substance is the essential part of you and that part of you is holiness. You are supposed to occupy your space with holiness. You are to be filled up with holiness and hold down the position in that state, because when satan comes looking, he should find holiness. If he does not find it, he and seven other demons are coming in . . . but not if holiness is there.

> "I beseech you therefore, brethren, by the mercies of God, that ye present your bodies a living sacrifice, holy, acceptable unto God, which is your reasonable service. And be not conformed to this world: but be ye transformed by the renewing of your mind."

Romans 12:1-2 may be a familiar Scripture for some of you, but I need you to read it again, for the first time. This is an earnest plea for you, who live for God, to present your body to Him as a living sacrifice, holy and acceptable, which is your reasonable service. It's only reasonable not only because of what God has done for you, but because you were created in holiness. It's only naturally reasonable for you to live holy. You are equipped and supplied with the ability to live holy. I still hear somebody saying, "You don't understand, it's hard." If you are saying that, you still have your doubts about God's power to deliver you.

We talked about how your spirit was the only part of you that was saved/recreated/born again. Well, what happened to the rest of you—your soul and your body? Your body will only be able to live a sacrificed, holy, and acceptable life for God **when you make up your mind to do it.** Your body will follow your mind. Your body did not get saved when you (your spirit) did, therefore, your body has to be transformed to holiness. Your body is used to living the way it wants to live, when it wants. It does not know a thing about holiness. Your body wants temporal, fast, sensuous pleasures. Your spirit and body are fighting, at war with each other. Your spirit is crying out to be what it naturally is, but it can't because Galatians 5:17 tells us that our bodies are fighting it, trying to take it to lay down in sin.

> "The old sinful nature loves to do evil, which is just opposite from what the Holy Spirit wants. And the Spirit gives us desires that are opposite from what the sinful nature desires. These two forces are constantly fighting each other, and your choices are never free from this conflict." (NLT)

Your spirit is saying, "Jesus rescued me from hell and we are going to live right for God. We will be pleasing to Him and live our life holy for Him. I don't want to go and lay where you are trying to take us. I don't lay in mess, I don't lie in a bed of sin, I don't lay in death." Your body is totally the opposite, "Look, spirit, forget all that foolishness you are talking about. I'm going to do what I feel like. I can't wait, I don't want to wait . . . I want it now. I've been doing what I want to do all this time and you are not going to come in here trying to be holier-than-thou, but you are going to go where I take you. We'll deal with the consequences later."

Guess where this fight is taking place? Your mind. Your mind is the battleground and what's in it will determine if your spirit will prevail or if your body will lay you down in sin. So, here you are, you have given your life to Christ, which immediately freed and rescued you from the bondage of sin, but your mind has prevented you from possessing it. You've obtained healing, wholeness, peace and deliverance, yet, you have past wounds that are not healed, your body is still detached and divided in parts, and your heart is still broken and in agony. **You've been rescued from hell, but still in bondage, and the chains that bind you are holding your mind captive to your past.**

How can a man or woman who has given his or her life to the omnipotent, all-powerful God through the spotless, uncontaminated Blood of Jesus Christ, be trapped, chained, and handcuffed to sin? Luke 11:17 tells us how:

"A house divided against itself will fall."

Can you imagine Evander Holyfield getting in a boxing ring and the announcer says, "In this corner, weighing two hundred sixty pounds, heavyweight champion of the world, Evannnnnnder Hoooooooolyfield! And in this corner, weighing in at two hundred sixty pounds, the undisputed champion of the world, Evannnnnnder Hooooooooolyfied!" The bell sounds "ding" and Holyfield starts punching himself in the face. It does not matter that your spirit is reborn; if your body and soul and mind are fighting against it, you will be TKO'd, conquered and defeated by sexual sin. Then sin will walk around again, holding you up in the air saying, "I'm the undisputed champion over you." Your spirit, soul, and body have to be in unison. You cannot give your spirit to God without your body and your mind. In fact, Matthew 22:37–38 tell us that this is God's greatest commandment—that you give your entire self to Him.

> "You must love the Lord your God with all your heart, all your soul, and all your mind. This is the first and greatest commandment."

Loving the Lord completely is the most essential part of your life. You can't have a reborn spirit that loves God, but have a mind that serves sin. In Hosea 4:6 God says that his people are destroyed because they lack knowledge, "They do not know Me." Let's distinguish something here. There are a lot of people who "know" Scriptures, who attend church; but the definition of the word "know" means to perceive or understand clearly and with certainty to the point of change. If there's no evidence of change, then, you only gathered information, not knowledge.

There's a quite a number of people who go to church out of habit or moral obligation, but in this same chapter of Hosea in verse ten, God says that when you seek satisfaction in other things instead of Him, you'll eat but you'll remain hungry. You can get temporal pleasure from it, but you will not be fulfilled. There's a lot of hungry, starving Christians in church. This is what separates you from those who have the title "Christian" but have not experienced or lived being one. Living for and serving God with all of your being, including your mind, a changed mind, is what prevents you from perishing. A renewed mind prevents you from going back to sexual sin. It's important to know that leaving contaminated relationships and changing your environment when you get saved is commendable, but understand that it is not enough. You can leave and still see no change. You can go to a new city or a new place, get into a new relationship and do the same things that you did in the previous ones.

You can only experience the fullness of God when you renew, change, and reclaim your mind. Your mind is conditioned to sin. You've developed a consistent pattern of immoral sexual activities. In the book of Numbers chapter thirteen and fourteen, you can see that God instantly delivered the children of Israel out of their bondage (Egypt) but it took forty years to deliver their minds. It has been proven that it would only take a few days to get to the Promised Land but their minds were programmed to live a life of bondage. Even though God had delivered them, their minds were still chained to their past. You've been delivered out of your bondage, but now, your mind has to be deprogrammed of the patterns you've developed while you were in bondage. It is up to you how long it will take to get to your Promised Land. You can wander around in the wilderness of singleness or you can do what's necessary to cross over.

According to your Bible, the way you deprogram or change yourself is by renewing your mind. The way you can live a holy, sacrificed, and acceptable life is through a transformed mind, because you are not changed until your mind is changed. You can say you are a Christian, but until your mind gives evidence to that, you will just continue to wear the title. This is why single people become enslaved to masturbation, homosexuality, and every form of fornication, because the mind, the will, is attached to the act. They were strongholds in your mind, and a "thought stronghold" has to be renewed by the Word of God. Your mind has to become what you are. It has to be reprogrammed to the holy man or woman that you already are. So, renewing the mind is not an option, it's vitally necessary.

"For those who are according to the flesh and are controlled by its unholy desires set their minds on and pursue those things which gratify the flesh, but those who are according to the Spirit and are controlled by the desires of the Spirit set their minds on and seek those things which gratify the [Holy] Spirit. Now the mind of the flesh [which is sense and reason without the Holy Spirit] is death [death that comprises all the miseries arising from sin . . . But the mind of the of the [Holy] Spirit is life and [soul] peace . . . [That is] because the mind of the flesh [with its carnal thoughts and purposes] is hostile to God, for it does not submit itself to God's law; indeed it cannot. So then those who are living the life of the flesh [catering to the appetites and impulses of their carnal nature] cannot please or satisfy God, or be acceptable to Him." Romans 8:5-8 (Amplified)

The carnal, fleshly mind is an enemy to God. It resists and is in direct conflict with the will of God. The carnal mind will fight against Him because it wants to live out the desires of your flesh. God will tell you that you are holy and pure but your flesh will try to remind you that you are the opposite by bringing the memories of what you did last week. This is why you will not be able to please God with a carnal mind; it is programmed to what you think is right, what you've been influenced by—your upbringing, news, media and contamination from the world. The carnal mind is totally against God and is determined to live out what it feels, regardless of God being God. It is flat-out rebellious! And if you don't change your mind, you will be God's enemy. And the last thing you want is to be God's enemy

> "This is war, and there is no neutral ground. If you're not on my side, you're the enemy; if you're not helping, you're making things worse." Matthew 12:30 (The Message)

The first thing that Jesus gave the forgiven adulterous woman was a maintenance plan. He did the same thing with you when He freed her, forgave her and delivered her. He said, "Sin no more." He didn't leave her with just that; He gave her a means of doing that. Jesus said in John 8:12, "Follow Me." In essence, He was saying, "I've forgiven and delivered you, now maintain that, follow Me. If you follow Me, you won't stumble back in someone else's bed, into adultery, through darkness, because I will be leading you." This was not just for the woman in the

Bible, but it was for those there who couldn't cast a stone because of their sins. Then the Message translation says that the Pharisees objected to the "follow Me plan." "All we have is Your word on this. We need more than this to go on." Jesus replied, "You're right that you only have my word, but you can depend on it being true."

The Word of God is your maintenance plan. It's your manual. Your car has a manual, your VCR even has a manual and instructions that tell you how to properly use, maintain and keep them. Certainly, you need one! Some of you have a question mark on your forehead like the Pharisee, "All we get is the Word to keep us from sexual sin?" You didn't think you were going to get an over-the-counter remedy or a 12-step program or strategy, did you? If you did get one, then, you would be self-reliant and think that you could keep you from sexual sin. That's the problem, trying to do it without God. It is only through Him that you can remain free of sexual sin. Your strategy is The Word . . . and you can depend on it!

You can depend on it because God does **nothing** without the Word, nothing. In fact, John 1:1 declares that God and the Word are one. They are the same. The Word contains the same power as the Blood of Jesus, which delivered you from hell. It is the Word that God Himself swears by; He's bound by it. It is perfect, it's been tried, proven and it can't fail. Since you've made Jesus Lord over your life, then, the Word has to be Lord over your life. The Word has to govern and be the final authority in your life. It has to be the basis of defining how you live, act, feel, move, and breathe. It is not an option or last result. And never, ever, doubt the power of God's Word.

"Don't you know that those who do wrong will have no share in the Kingdom of God? Don't fool yourselves. Those who indulge in sexual sin, who are idol worshiper, adulterers, male prostitutes, homosexuals . . . none of these will have a share in the Kingdom of God. There was a time when some of you were just like that, but now your sins have been washed away, and you have been set apart of God. You have been made right with God because of what the Lord Jesus Christ and the Spirit of our God have done for you. You may say, "I am allowed to do anything." But I reply, "Not everything is good for you." And even though "I am allowed to do anything," I must not become a slave to anything." 1 Corinthians 6:9–12 (NLT)

Just because everybody else is "doing it," that condoms supposedly makes sex safe, that other people who attend church kiss someone they are not married to in the mouth, does not mean that it is right for you. **Just because it's good does not make it right.** It does not mean that God approves of it. I have heard many people who love God say that they don't feel anything is wrong with some of their carnal habits, "I don't **feel** anything's wrong with spending the night over my boyfriend's house." You can't continue to be ruled by your feelings. You have to make a decision that the Word of God will be the final authority and not your emotions.

"You know the next commandment pretty well, too: "Don't go to bed with another's spouse." But don't think you've preserved your virtue simply by staying out of bed. Your heart can be corrupted by lust even quicker than your body. Those leering looks you think nobody notices—they also corrupt. Let's not pretend this is easier than it really is, If you want to live a morally pure life, here's what you have to do: You have to blind your right eye the moment you catch it in a lustful leer." Matthew 5:27–30 (The Message)

You have to begin weighing <u>everything</u> –the physical as well as the mental-in your life by the Word. You are no longer self-contained, but you are to be kept by God's Word. The Word is clear that you will not be able to lay in someone's arms without being tempted or worse, having sex with them. Your Father is not trying to burden you down with rules. He's trying to keep you from hot coals, out of satan's territory, and into the parameters of safety.

This is why the Word of God should not be put to debate or to a contest with any other opinion to determine what are the best answers and solutions, for the Word is the **only** solution. It protects you and looks out for what is best for you because it is not separate from God; it is God and God is the only solution. And just as you are in the image and are patterned after God, then you are in the image of the Word. Open and hold your Bible up to you, look into it. This is your "mirror." Your life now has to reflect what's in it. It's your pattern for imitating God.

"The law of the LORD is perfect, converting the soul." Psalms 19:7

Convert means to change into a different form, to alter, or transform from one nature into another. This is how the change, the transformation of the mind, takes place through the Word. This is the means of presenting your body as a living sacrifice, holy and acceptable to God.

Do you look in the mirror every day? Of course, you do. You have to use the mirror every day to do the basic essentials—comb your hair, wash your face and brush your teeth. But no matter how good you look on the outside, if the inward man has not taken a daily look in the "mirror," you are dressed up for disaster! One of the problems that I see with many people who love God is a lack of discipline and inconsistency. That lack of discipline correlates to a lack of self-control.

> "For the Lord sees clearly what a man does, examining every path he takes. An evil man is held captive by his own sins; they are ropes that catch and hold him. He will die for lack of self-control; he will be lost because of his incredible folly." Proverbs 5:21–23

It is a man's lack of control that leads him to sin, which traps him and leads him right to destruction. The Message translation says that death is the reward for an undisciplined life and for making foolish decisions. You constantly have to make decisions every day and those decisions are made in the soulish realm, the mind. If your mind is not renewed daily by the Word, you are simply making foolish decisions. You will make decisions based on your emotions and thoughts that have been seduced and influenced by your contact with the world. You will make a decision based on what you feel and not based on what is real—the Word.

First things first, break the patterns and habits of yesterday. Psychologists say that it takes 21 days to form a habit and 3 days to break it. Your consistency will be key. You must know that renewing the mind will not take 21 days. It's a lifetime process. Many want to know when did my deliverance manifest, well the answer is: today! **Deliverance is daily.** This process never ends. Once delivered is not always delivered. You can't live off of last year's testimony. You have to put into practice the Word of God *daily!* You are influenced daily; you have to be renewed daily. The deprogramming stage is not one of the most asy and pleasant processes. Change is not easy and it can be uncomfortable, but it's necessary!

That's why you do not see everyone readily raising their hand, "Me, me, me . . . I'll change, I'll change." The right way, God's way, seems the hardest thing to do. It's easy to take the sinful way out, there's not much effort behind it. Sin is sitting up waiting to be used. That is why sin is an expression of cowardice; it takes a man or a woman of courage to do what's right. Holiness has to become a habit, and habits are birthed through discipline. In order for holiness to become a habit, you will have to discipline yourself to take daily actions on it. Again, consistency is key. I read a survey that said that about fifty percent of adults attend religious services at least once a week. There are about 2,015,000 Christians globally. I guess it's safe to say that there are people who know that they *need* God—or, it's either we are going, out of a moral obligation, or keeping up with family tradition. This is nothing new. When Jesus walked the earth, multitudes showed up at church. The problem is not getting folks there, it's getting them to live what they heard, after they leave, and to actually apply the Word.

"And again He began to teach by the sea. And a great multitude was gathered to Him, so that He got into a boat and sat in it on the sea; and the whole multitude was on the land facing the sea. Then He taught them many things by parables, and said to them in His teaching: "Listen! Behold, a sower went out to sow. And it happened, as he sowed, that some seed fell by the wayside; and the birds of the air came and devoured it. Some fell on stony ground, where it did not have much earth; and immediately it sprang up because it had no depth of earth. But when the sun was up it was scorched, and because it had no root it withered away. And some seed fell among thorns; and the thorns grew up and choked it, and it yielded no crop. But other seed fell on good ground and yielded a crop that sprang up, increased and produced: some thirtyfold, some sixty, and some a hundred." And He said to them, "He who has ears to hear, let him hear!" But when He was alone, those around Him with the twelve asked Him about the parable. And He said to them, "To you it has been given to know the mystery of the kingdom of God; but to those who are outside, all things come in parables, so that 'Seeing they may see and not perceive, And hearing they may hear and not understand; Lest they should turn, And their sins be forgiven them.'" Mark 4:1–12

Here, you have Jesus preaching a sermon by way of a parable to a large congregation. I can imagine their confused faces, "What in the world is He talking about?" After the Benediction, a few of them took Jesus to the side to ask Him to explain.

"And He said to them, "Do you not understand this parable? How then will you understand all the parables? The sower sows the word. And these are the ones by the wayside where the word is sown. When they hear, Satan comes immediately and takes away the word that was sown in their hearts. These likewise are the ones sown on stony ground who, when they hear the word, immediately receive it with gladness; and they have no root in themselves, and so endure only for a time. Afterward, when tribulation or persecution arises for the word's sake, immediately they stumble. [18]Now these are the ones sown among thorns; they

are the ones who hear the word, and the cares of this world, the deceitfulness of riches, and the desires for other things entering in choke the word, and it becomes unfruitful. But these are the ones sown on good ground, those who hear the word, accept it, and bear fruit: some thirtyfold, some sixty, and some a hundred."
Mark 4:13-20

The scripture shows four types of Christians. The first type is the one who goes to church, leaves right afterwards and goes back to the *way* he/she lived before, commonly known as the Wayside Christian. This is usually the type of person who "attends" church, hears the Word, but will never live by it. They still allow satan to have rule over their life because right after they hear the Word, satan walks right up to them, snatches the Word and says, "I'll take that. You have no use for it. It does not line up with the plans that I have for you."

Then, you have the Stony Christian, who hears the Word, shouts, runs up and down the church aisle and uses phrases that sound like this, "Girl, that Word was good. He was preachin'! That Word was powerful!" But as soon as the time comes for them to act on the Word, they opt to do what they did while they were in the world instead. The word that comes to mind when I think of a Stony Christian is the word rock—back and forth, in and out. One day, a mountain, the next day, a pebble . . . I'm with Jesus today, but tomorrow, I don't want to be a Christian. There is no consistency; you are living a double life. And a double-minded man is unstable in all his ways.

> "For a doubtful mind is as unsettled as a wave of the sea that is driven and tossed by the wind. People like that should not expect to receive anything from the Lord. They can't make up their minds. They waver back and forth in everything they do…And remember, it is a message to obey, not just to listen to. If you don't obey, you are only fooling yourself. For if you just listen and don't obey, it is like looking at your face in a mirror but doing nothing to improve your appearance. You see yourself, walk away,

and forget what you look like. But if you keep looking steadily into God's perfect law--the law that sets you free--and if you do what it says and don't forget what you heard, then God will bless you for doing it." James 1:6b–8, 22–24 (NLT)

Thirdly, you have the Thorny Christian, the dangerous type. Almost like the Stony Christian, but they are more dangerous because they're the kind you cannot trust. You see, the Stony Christian just needs some stick-to-it-ness consistency to be dedicated—that the trial is only temporary—and to simply trust God at His Word. But Mr. Thorny, on the other hand, will quote a Scripture, sing worship music and then sleep with the pastor's wife. Yeah, they want to keep up with the Joneses and climb up ladders so bad, that they'll kick you off the ladder to get ahead, while at the same time they'll say, "God bless you . . . Praise God . . . God is Good . . . Blessed is the city . . . Money cometh to me . . ." But little do they know, they are going to get jabbed and choked by their own thorns.

Last, but certainly not the least, is Good Ground. This is the type of Christian that we all you need to be: one who hears the Word, acts on it, and then receives God's blessings. The Bible is a working document in their lives; it's not left in the car until next Sunday or sitting on the coffee table at home collecting dust. They are faithfully meditating on the Word daily, responding to it in faith. "Trials come, no problem, God's Word will prevail . . . I'm low on money, I have needs that need to be met, but I will not use the tithe or sleep with someone for money." They will not need to kick someone off the ladder because they know God is in the business of promoting. When temptations come, God will make a way of escape and they'll respond to it. A person planted on good ground will always prevail and overcome any situation.

Now, out of 2,015,000 Christians, how many do you think are on good ground? Probably only twenty-five percent; the other seventy-five percent are made up of Wayside, Thorny and Stony

Christians. This is why Jesus said, if you don't understand this parable in Mark 4, you will not understand any other parable. In other words, He was saying this is the most important of them all, because if you don't have the Word, your ground will crumble from underneath you.

There are multitudes of people who show up at church on Sunday mornings, but only twenty-five percent are really committing themselves to God. Millions of people go right into church and leave back out the same way. And it's not because of God or because the Word is not going forth. It's because we are not living it. If you don't have the Word, I promise you that you will fail. You can't operate in or understand any other parable if you don't get this one. The Word of God is the foundation for every believer's life and if you do not live by it, you'll be like the other seventy-five percent—just church-goers. It's not a temporary, part-time thing, when you feel like it (I'll get to it when I get to it). It's a full-time, permanent way of life. Get determined to get all of what God has for you . . . Get into the Word daily!

I have seen many people go to jail for a crime that they did not commit, but planned to commit. This is called conspiracy. You can get as much time for plotting to do something wrong just as if you had perpetrated the crime. It does not matter if you never get to the bank and steal a quarter. The fact that you are planning it already makes you a thief. You have a getaway plan, the clothes you will wear are picked carefully (you don't want to create any attention or your identity revealed). You have the map of the bank, you know where the safe deposit is, and you also have a weapon.

Let's look in the "mirror" again. In the book of Mark, you have the Pharisees, who taught the law but did not live it, trying to check Jesus because he did not wash His hands before He ate a piece of chicken. It was one of the traditions that the Pharisees kept. Big Brother Jesus told them that they were hypocrites because they honored God by proclaiming Him with their mouth, but not in heart or action. There are many Pharisees in the church today who wear their church hats on Sunday, sing "Amazing Grace" (how sweet the sound), shout and run down the aisles, take up communion . . . but curse, drink, lie and sleep around with folks they are not married to. That's not communion, you just took a sip of some grape juice; you had an early morning snack. The Bible says that this is why you see Christians prematurely dying . . . because they are playing church out of tradition. Shoutin' on Sunday, but useless on Monday.

> "And then He added, "It is the thought-life that defiles you. For from within, out of a person's heart, come evil thoughts, sexual immorality . . . adultery . . . wickedness, deceit, eagerness for lustful pleasure. All these vile things come from within; they are what defile you and make you unacceptable to God." Mark 7:20–23 (NLT)

The word heart is translated the mind. Out of your mind, where your thought life exists, comes sexual immorality. Your thoughts cause you to become impure. Any action in your life started out as a thought. You thought about it, then, you acted on it. In essence, as declared in Proverbs 23:7, you are your thoughts, "As a man thinketh, so is he." Your thoughts are just as powerful as your actions. In order to end the vicious cycle of sexual sin, you need to change what you've been thinking about. Your old thoughts have to be replaced with new thoughts in order for you to have pure actions.

"For though we walk in the flesh, we do not war after the flesh: (For the weapons of our warfare are not carnal, but mighty through God to the pulling down of strong holds;) Casting down imaginations, and every high thing that exalteth itself against the knowledge of God, and bringing into captivity every thought to the obedience of Christ." II Corinthians 10:3-5

The weapons, the devices that you use to get rid of or cast imaginations and thoughts out are not carnal (not people— earthly, worldly, or mentally), but it is through God. We have established that God is His Word, so that means that your device to get rid of lustful, unholy, ungodly thoughts or imaginations is the Word. The Amplified translation says that the Word, your weapon against lustful thoughts, is mighty before God in overthrowing and destroying strongholds. Anything that has paralyzed your mind can be overthrown and destroyed through the Word. Not only thoughts, but arguments, theories, reasoning and every proud and lofty thing that sets itself up against or tries to elevate above the knowledge of God or the Word, should be overthrown and destroyed. So, when you have a thought, impression, question, or when a debate arises, you have to take that lustful thought and replace it or overthrow it with the Word.

This, again, tells you why you have to look in the "mirror" daily to determine if a belief or thought is contrary to the Word and to know what to replace an ungodly image with. Okay, let's try it. I learned this years ago, through an awesome man of God, Dr. Creflo Dollar. Think of a tornado, of dark clouds and lightning, of high winds blowing, trees falling down, debris and large pieces of wood blowing everywhere. Now, count to ten. What happened to the image of the tornado? The counting overthrew it. This is the same action you must take when you get an unholy thought or image in your mind: open you mouth and speak the Word of God. You don't sit there and ponder on or rehearse the thought, you cast it out. If you don't cast it out, you'll act it out!

Every time the thought comes, "You should call him. You are stressed out; you need to be held." Don't meditate on the thought and picture yourself picking up the phone and start rehearsing what you are going to wear for him and say to him. No, cast it out, "God, you are holy, therefore, I am holy. I am made in your image. You wouldn't lie down with satan nor do what he does, neither will I. The Word is not devoid of power, neither am I. I have the Word of God on the inside of me, that gives me the power to overcome, overthrow, dismantle, and destroy my thoughts or any ungodly desire that tries to exalt itself above You or tries to prevent me from doing Your will. I don't need someone to hold me, I am held by you, Lord, and Your Word. The Holy Spirit comforts and keeps me. [When I'm] weak, I am strong. It is your sufficient Grace that kee[ps me. I can] do any and all things through Christ who gives me the [strength to] do it. The Word is my shield, my buckler and I'm tying it on tight. It shields me from sinning against my Father. You said that if Your Word, Lord, abides in me, then You would abide in me. Your Word keeps me pure and from contamination. Because Your Word abides in me, I can ask anything and it is granted. I am holy. I am kept. I am celibate in and through the mighty name of Jesus!"

Open up your mouth and proclaim 1 Peter 1:15, Isaiah 55:11, 2 Corinthians 12:10, John 14:16, John 15:1–3, Psalms 18:30, Philippians 4:13, Psalms 119:140, and Proverbs 30:5. That's right, you have to get fierce and declare the Word of God over your life because the devil is not playing with you. He's mad about it, he wants you back and he'll do anything to get you back . . . at whatever cost. So, you have to be on guard and take control of your thoughts because this is where satan operates—in your thought life and in your desires and emotions. Oh, and satan is coming back, even after you have cast the thought out; he does not just come and tempt you one time. If he did it to Jesus, he'll do it to you. Ungodly thoughts will plague your mind and make you think you are not saved, that you have not been forgiven, and that you are not holy. Everybody gets tempted, **everybody**. When temptation comes my way, I'll say, "Daddy, if you don't get that fine man away from me . . ."

Just because you get a thought does not mean that you are not holy, but not casting it out can cause you to act on impure sexual desires and sins. Like a conspiracy, you have to get a hold of your thoughts and make a plan to be holy. Think about it and think about it; make a plot to be pure. "This is what I'm going to do when satan comes in my thoughts, I'm going to do and say this. When Ray tries to come back into my life, I'm going to do this. When Tina tries to call me, I'm going to say . . ." Have your getaway plan, "I'm not wearing that shirt anymore or those pants because it shows or reveals my identity." Pull out your map, the Bible, because you'll need a weapon. Go into the safety deposit and pull out holiness. Yes, you have to purposely plan and plot your holiness. Meditate and think about how you are going to execute it. It's the conspiracy theory. Get caught being holy.

To be caught holy means that you need to be active in holiness at all times. Holiness has to become a habit and habits are birthed through discipline. In order for holiness to become a habit, you will have to discipline yourself to take daily actions in it. Again, consistency is key. But even with consistency and all the right answers, you still need God's grace.

"Nothing in all creation is hidden from God's sight. Everything is uncovered and laid bare before the eyes of him to whom we must give account. Therefore, since we have a great high priest who has gone through the heavens, Jesus the Son of God, let us hold firmly to the faith we profess. For we do not have a high priest who is unable to sympathize with our weaknesses, but we have one who has been tempted in every way, just as we are--yet was without sin. Let us then approach the throne of grace with confidence, so that we may receive mercy and find grace to help us in our time of need." Hebrews 4:13–16 (NLT)

You have to boldly take your position and operate under God's grace and the Word, to overcome your struggle and maintain deliverance. We all have weaknesses and struggles we are trying to overcome and Jesus knows this because He was tempted, yet He never submitted to the temptation. He knows the means of withstanding the temptations, so you don't have to go to God with insecurity when you are weak and plagued with thoughts or shortcomings. Receive His mercy and the grace that He is ready to give you. As you take a look in the "mirror" daily, you will begin to see your life transform right before your eyes, but it's going to take commitment and diligence to see the change. Stay on the job, full time, and you'll see that the pay and benefits outweigh any position you'll ever stand in. You have the best boss in the world and the retirement plan is like no other . . . Stay committed!

Chapter Seven: Healing Your Heart

"I am worn out from sobbing. Every night tears drench my bed; my pillow is wet from weeping." Psalms 6:6 NLT

There's nothing worse than having a pain you can't stop. I'd be happy to take a pill from a bottle for the pain, but even if I did, it would only medicate me. It would blanket the pain, but before long it would come back. That temporary blanket somehow covers me and many wouldn't even know that I was suffering- and I could even fool myself sometimes. I'd be fine, going on with my 'daily usuals' and bang! Out of no where the symptoms would creep up on me again and I'd be back in a fetal position, trying to stomach the pain. Sound familiar? Been there, done that, bought the t-shirt and want to take it back and get your money?

As I go around the world from city to city, state to state preaching, all too often I see people like you, and once me, blanketing their pain. Lip-stick-plastered, painted on smiles, suited up with a Donna Karen dress, a fabricated hallelujah and a clichéd "Oh, I'm blessed and highly favored" salutation covers up all their wounds. Oh, I looked good on the outside, too, but there was an internal conflict and all the while I really wanted to release one of those kinds of cries from the belly where you're snoting and carrying on and screaming, *"No! I'm really not fine! I'm not doing well at all! I'm hurting on the inside, I don't feel like I can make it through this, the pain in unbearable. I'm afraid to tell anybody for fear of how they may think of me or that it ends up in the church bulletin...I don't have it all together. Everything's falling apart, I don't know what to do and don't even think I have the strength to do it if I did know what to do. I've failed God and can't face Him. I have no one to talk to and I'm forced to suffer with this on my own…I'm depressed, my esteem has suffered a low, I feel like I'm going out of my mind, My job is being affected by this, and so are the kids, I can't sleep, I can't eat…"*

Instead, the plastered smile forms, then a "Girl, I'm blessed" leaves my lips, and the 'Great Pretend Game' begins. There were many times that I had to drag myself out of that fetal position and force my way to church, but you would never know because my make-up concealed my tear-stained face. And those tears during worship service were not from 'praising the Lord'…those tears were evidence of my struggle. People thought because I showed up for church that I was alright. I had only put a band-aid on a bullet wound. Church was part of my regular routine, it became the norm for me. I did the mid-week Bible study, early- morning prayer, I was on a first name basis with the 'veteran Christians' and I didn't even have to use the table of contents to find the book of Habakkuk. I thought I was delivered. I thought I was healed from the molestation, abortion and even from the broken hearts I had suffered. I hadn't "slipped" and slept with anyone in a very long time. But time only passed, it didn't heal.

You've heard it, people say that all the time, "Time heals". Well, time was moving and the clock was ticking, but I was not really dealing with the pain and the hurt; I was just covering it up. This bears repeating: **time never heals, God does.** Time is nothing without God; an empty hour, with useless minutes. Now, God will use time, but time never does the healing, He does. I was only medicating myself with pretend pills because I used time to do 'God-activities' without God. Oh, I had the healed "look"; cleaned up on the outside. The pretense was clothed in religious acts by showing up to church and quoting scriptures. I may not have had open wounds and scars visible to the eye, but you can be sure, there was internal bleeding. I was bleeding and didn't even know it. I was dying on the inside.

"Why does it hurt so bad" was the song of my life. My everyday life sang that song over and over again, can we take my life off of repeat. I was frustrated, time after time, the same cycle; different man, same results, different hotel, same effect, different bed, different sheets, same wounds. It got to the point as if I had gone on a diet, doing well, working out, changed my eating habits, but now I'm binging and eating Snickers candy bars and Big Macs. And the nerve to super size it with a diet coke! I would go a while and not fall to the enemy's sex trap, going to church, doing the "saved" stuff, reading my Bible but then, bam! I would go on a binge and super size the sin. Because once you fall, it gets worse, as if you've never been saved or delivered. But I would have my diet coke. Oh, yeah, I didn't stop going to church, I just incorporated my sex binge with worship.

"Master, which is the great commandment in the law? Jesus said unto him, Thou shalt love the Lord thy God with all thy heart, and with all thy soul, and with all thy mind. This is the first and great commandment." Matthew 22:36-38

You couldn't tell me that I wasn't keeping the great commandment. I did everything you just read in the previous chapters. I was casting down the thoughts, renewing my mind, changed my sinning friends, turned off the bump and grind music, consistently attending church, you name it, I did it. I couldn't figure out how I ended up over his house, though! Okay, I'm here now; I'll just use a condom and repent later. There was no condom on the shelf that could protect me from what was about to happen to my spirit or my heart. So every time I went on my sex binge, another wound would be punctured. Every time I had illegal sex it left a scar on my memory and I continued to rehearse it over and over again in my life. You rewind the sexual experience all over again and even the pain attached to it. I don' know about you, but I got tired of the re-runs. Please, somebody, change the channel! So I did. I would repent again, say I wasn't going to do it anymore, I wasn't going to see him again, but then my life started singing the song again.

I was keeping the great commandment, yeah right! How could I, when someone else had my heart? How could I, when my heart was broken? How could I love God with all my mind, when it was always on someone else? How could I possibly love God with all my soul, when it was still tied in other places? I coerced myself into thinking that I was okay because I began to touch without feeling and I became desensitized in church services. I began to believe the lie that I could just go and have sex to fulfill the empty places in me and it would not affect me. All the while sin was affecting my hearing. I could sit right in church right next to the Christian I slept with the night before. I wish somebody would just let me tell the truth! I was a backslider with a membership card. I was empty. No, I wasn't dying on the inside, I was just about dead. I was not healed, I was broken and I had only covered up the pain and my wounded heart.

One thing I know is that I wanted it and I wanted it bad and I was willing to do whatever to get it! I wanted to be healed. I wanted my heart to be put back together again and I didn't want to go down the same yellow brick road again to see the wizard but I sincerely wanted the Lord to give me a new heart and make me whole. But how could I when I had a memory seared by sexual sin? Oh, I questioned my sincerity. Did I really want to walk away from this? Was God paying me back for my sins? Did He really forgive me? Did I *really* repent? I admit, there were times that I had apologized, but this time I was for real. I didn't want to live a life of a counterfeit Christian anymore. Coming to church faking it like me and Jesus were cool; knowing that I wasn't living right. Knowing that I was struggling and tormented in my mind. In the middle of service, and get a flashback of someone climbing up on the top of me. "I'm tired of living like this, it's killing me. I don't want to live a lie anymore, I'm taking off this mask and I don't care what's exposed. I want the residue of every sexual act stripped off of me. Erase the painful memory of it, Lord. I'm tired of every time that the memory comes up, I go and relive it. Kill it from the root this time, Lord, remove the fingerprints. AND LORD, STOP THE BLEEDING! DO INTERNAL SURGERY AND HEAL MY HEART!"

I go in many 'Emergency room-Churches' filled with hurting, hemorrhaging Christians with a trail of blood following them and altar calls filled with injured people responding to God's invitation to do internal surgery. I receive thousands of emails from sexually damaged Christians from around the world, crying out, "how do I stop this, how do I get out of this relationship, how can I really live my life for the Lord, what I do with these sexual urges?" I'm here to tell you, there is no pill in a bottle and cold showers don't work. Putting a teaspoon of cold water on a blazing, hot fire does nothing but make the fire burn hotter. What you need is urgent care. What takes place during illegal sex requires a skillful surgeon to cut away the damage without killing you. And I have just the Surgeon for you.

"God means what he says, What he says goes, His powerful Word is sharp as a surgeon's scalpel, cutting through everything, whether doubt or defense, laying us open to listen and obey." Hebrews 4:12 (The Message)

"For the Word that God speaks is alive and full of power [making it active, operative, energizing, and effective]; it is sharper than any two edged sword, penetrating to the dividing line of the breath of life (soul) and [the immortal] spirit, and of joints and marrow [of the deepest parts of our nature] exposing and sifting and analyzing and judging the very thoughts and purposes of the heart." Amplified Version

The Word is so powerful that it does corrective surgery on us, cutting away at anything that hinders us from serving the Lord wholeheartedly. It cuts away at our uncertainty, excuses, and questions so that it may open us up to God's revelation about our situation and to give us the power and the ability to come out of our state of affairs with victory. The Word of God examines and investigates our flesh and judges its intentions. It separates our spirit from any conflicting intellect and wavering emotions so that it may open us up to God's truths. In essence, the Word of God reveals our fickle emotions, exposes what condition we're really in, and then filters out what is inconsistent or contrary to the Word.

Consequently, the Word examines your heart, it examines your soul and it examines your mind and judges its thoughts, plans and intentions. God in His great wisdom created your entire body to function and intermingle with its members. And He designed you in mind that your whole life would glorify Him and be used for and by Him. Let me give you an example. Each part of your body has a purpose or function, whether it be your eyes with optic nerves, or hands with fingers, feet with toes, a tongue with taste buds and nerve endings that produce saliva. You don't know how it all works, but when you tell your brain to lift your hands, it does. Go ahead, tell your brain to make your eyelids blink. Whoa! Cool, huh? Okay, you maybe thinking that's corny because you are so use to your brain functioning that way on an everyday basis that you don't even think about it, you just do it. But when you really think about it, God is just a genius, a Mastermind! No pun intended but He created your brain to help work and engineer your body. He would never give you a commandment or require you to do something that He didn't give you the ability to do. He would never obligate you to love Him with all your heart (spirit), all your soul (emotions), with all your mind (intellect), with all your strength (physically) without filling you with the capacity to do it.

Telling your brain to move your fingers is one thing, but it's another thing to tell your brain to love someone! Hey, before you tell your heart when and who to love, you should know that God created your brain, both male and female, with a natural hormone called oxytocin. Interestingly so, it comes from the Greek meaning 'swift birth'. This chemical is produced in the brain and is naturally released in a woman during child birth by stimulating uterine contractions. This oxytocin in the brain sends messages to woman's breast so that it releases milk for the mother to breast feed. Moreover, the mother is wired with this natural chemical to create a strong emotional bond between her and the baby. So, not only does God create you with the ability to love Him but you also have a built in capacity to love others. Cooler than having your brain make your eyes blink, huh?

Even more intriguing is the fact that oxytocin is commonly called the 'cuddle hormone' because of its ability to help men and women form strong emotional bonds. When released in the brain, oxytocin works in the blood, where it travels to tissues and nerve fibers in your body where it regulates body temperature, blood pressure, wound healing and even relief from pain, as well as learning and memory. Okay, here's what really gets me. This hormone is naturally released in response to cervical stimulation during sex and is also released during sexual orgasm, thus, creating a bond with the person you have sex with. To add to that, a doctor noted that the release of oxytocin can be conditioned, so after repeatedly having sex with this sex partner, just seeing that partner could release more oxytocin, making you want to be with that person all the more, and you bond. Simply put, they become addicted to each other through a process of sexual imprinting as these chemicals are released in the body. This doctor went on to say, "It's like this, you first meet him and he's passable. The second time you go out with him, he's OK. The third time you go out with him, you have sex. And from that point on, you can't imagine what life would be like without him."

If you think oxytocin is something, get a load of this! There is another natural hormone in your brain called dopamine responsible in conveying messages of euphoria, cravings and addiction to the brain. Talk about a natural high! This chemical also provides feelings of reinforcement to motivate you to do or continue an activity, while at the same time making you feel good about doing it. So, when a man has sex it feels good to him because of the dopamine that's released. He has a strong feeling of happiness, confidence and well being. He comes to the notion that sex is enjoyable and dopamine causes him to seek out more of it based on how it happened the first time. He can become psychologically dependent upon sex where it's always on his mind and then he begins to form a compulsive habit. He's now ruled by his emotions and when the craving comes along, he feeds it. He then develops an obsession and he'll use whatever means to satisfy his sexual appetite: masturbation, pornography, multiple sex partners, you name it. The spirit of lust now engulfs him because of his uncontrollable, inordinate desire for sex. Large dosage of dopamine has him on serious high.

A psychologist stated that the aftermath of lustful sex is similar to the result of taking opiates (drugs that soothe your feelings, induces sleep or to stupefy). Stupefied? That definitely describes the after effects. Then, a stimulating combination of chemical changes occurs, including increases in serotonin, oxytocin, vasopressin and endogenous opioids. All big lettered-words that are probably making your head spin, but stick with me, I'm going somewhere. Now, serotonin is a chemical in the body that controls the body's cycle. It plays a role in preventing the body from going into depression, impulsive or uncontrollable behavior, and mood disorders. Without it you'd probably be "snap, crackle, pop". Then, vasopressin is a natural hormone partly responsible for recalling events and enhancing memory imprints. Finally, the 17 lettered endogenous opioids, which is the body's natural equivalent of heroin. This chemical is a natural pain killer in the body but when you violate and abuse a natural process, a chemical imbalance is the result.

With anything you abuse, and yes, even sex, a tolerance level develops and you have to use more sex to achieve the same intensity of the previous 'high'. And the higher the sex dosage, the physical dependence and addiction develops and despite reason or logic, the behavior is continued. When the effect of lust-filled sex wears off the dopamine level falls, the user experiences the reduced level as a depressed mood and then will 're-use' in order to re-establish the 'high'. Now you have adapted to the presence of lust-filled sex and at this point withdrawal symptoms will occur if you reduce or stop the sexual acts. To reverse an addiction is painful and this is one of the main reasons why people stay addicted: to avoid going through the painful state of withdrawal. With the chemical imbalance, instead of your body maintaining its proper mental balance, you are now having uncontrollable behavior, mood swings, up and down, living churchy one day, then stretch out in somebody else's bed the next. Every time you think that you are back on track, vasopressin vividly recalls him putting his tongue down your mouth. And because this chemical enhances memory imprints, it will recall the sexual acts when you smell their perfume or cologne. It will cause you to remember words that were spoken. The recall button is pushed when you hear a song replayed, see, touch or taste anything linked with the sexual encounter.

This even goes back to the tongue kissing and dating. A cycle of casual dating places you in what I call trial marriages, where you audition for marriage and try out the experiences and each encounter leave you with imprints that you carry with you. These chemicals are released in the brain when you tongue kiss someone and traces of that person and the experience is released in your saliva. When two people are standing at the altar to unite in matrimony, they commit their vows to one another, they are pronounced as husband and wife, and then the minister/priest says, "Now you may kiss the bride." The word 'now' is a key word; up until now you were not entitled to touch her until you committed your life to her. When you tongue kiss someone you are not married to, you are prematurely bonding with them, entering into a covenant; giving the chemical in your brain permission to rehearse or recall that touch and the feeling attached to it.

This recall can even take place even if you've switched partners because humans are widely conditioned by their sexual and social experiences. Because of this conditioning, you'll often find that people develop a tendency to date the same type of person and they'll even leave a failed relationship but begin dating that same person just with a different name. It is said that researchers think that people develop a 'love map' as they grow up. The experiences you encounter are designed and layered brick by brick and these bricks contain what you come to know as "attractiveness". It becomes wired in your desire. She says, "Roses, dinner and rent money means he loves me; He says, "Commitment? I've paid the meal and the bill and its time to get a return on my investment." It'll happen with out hesitation, you'll meet someone and the chemicals in your brain will try to live out what you've conditioned it to and it will attempt to recapture those moments; good or bad.

Quite often you'll find people in what I call "transitional relationships". Transitional relationships are affairs covered in co-dependency solely for the use of keeping a person from going through the 'withdrawal' stages. Okay, after one sexual relationship ends the dopamine level falls, the brain says, "hey, what happened to my thrill?" Your emotions then go into a whirl spin, then dives to a low depression and the withdrawal symptoms surface. Because oxytocin bonds like super glue, the tearing or pulling away is an agonizing, excruciating pain. So, it's either painfully withdraw from the sexual dependency or transit to another sexual relationship and re-establish the 'high'…did I hear you say you'll pick the transitional relationship?

I believe I did because there are many of you, right now, reading this book with sexual wounds, in relationships that are killing you, tormented by your past and under attack in your mind, struggling with bouts of depression and loneliness, trapped in sexual affairs that you are afraid to walk away from, postponing the detox stage in hopes of finding that 'special someone' so that you will not have to go through the withdrawals. If you are bleeding now, walking down the isle won't change that. If you are a whoremonger now, you'll be a whoremonger in the marriage. Changing your marital status will not stop the bleeding. Marriage is not deliverance! Nor is it a healing ministry. If you are expecting your spouse to heal your wounds, you are sadly mistaken because God will never give you someone who will replace Him. He is your healer.

"He heals the brokenhearted and binds up their wounds curing their pains and their sorrows." Psalms 147:3

This is God's will, not only for you to be delivered, but healed. The word bind means to heal. He does not want to put a band-aid on the wound but He wants to heal your wounds and your broken heart; not to medicate the pain but to cure it. To cure means to dismantle the very source of the pain and to restore to health. Listen, Believer, you have a God-given, Blood-bought right to be healed and made whole! The enemy may have wounded and left you for dead, but he messed up, he should have never left you with a pulse! Because one breath from God will restore your life! Do you hear me? I said the Lord can breathe on you and everything destructive in your life will come to naught! Zero! Zilch! Nothing! Whatever is causing the bleeding will be cut off at its root. Understand this, Exodus 34:14 affirms that God is a jealous God. No, the Word says scratch that, I'm not a jealous God, my name is Jealous. God will not allow anything and no one to take His place in your life. He will protect, guard, and even kill to have you; to be first place in your life. Oh, you don't think so? He even allowed His Son to be crucified just so that He can spend eternity with you. He is out of His mind in love with you and it hurts His heart to see you torn apart; especially because of bondage and some sexual stronghold! Oh, no, not when He is supposed to be your Stronghold! The Lord declares in Psalms 18 that He is your Deliverer and your Stronghold. "I hold that position in your life and nothing and no one is to have a hold on you like that but Me! I am the One that you are to love with all your heart, all your mind, and all your soul, and yes, your body is mine, so much so, that I chose to live there in it."

Oh, come on, some of you have had a jealous lover before; they are crazy! Parked outside your house all night, always want to spend time with you, constantly holding your hand in public to ensure everyone knows you belong to them, calling you every five minutes, questioning you, "Who is over there, where ya been all day, where did you get that shirt from, who bought it for you? I buy your things…" Just crazy! And God said, "That's just how I am about you. I want you for myself and I'm not willing to share anyone with you unless they are willing to enter into a covenant with you like I did." Yes, crazy in love with you! He wants to provide all your needs, fulfill your desires, provide your healing and let it be known to everyone that you are His; protecting and watching over you constantly. All He wants is for you to love Him in return.

It's His greatest commandment. He created you with the ability to do it. Love uses these very chemicals to cause you to bond with an addiction to God, causing you to stick to Him like super glue, igniting a thirst and a craving for an even more satisfying relationship with Him. He placed these natural hormones in your brain so that you could recall the memories that you made with Him; memory imprints of His unconditional love for you and to remind you of all the other times that He was there for you. Depression? Please! Not when your mind would be engrafted with His peace as it rehearsed over and over His goodness. Loneliness? Never! When the chemicals in your brain would remind you of the last time He held you in His comforting arms, followed by another chemical recall of the many times when He spoke in your ear, "I'll never leave you nor forsake you." And because love never fails or ceases, but continues to give and grow, He engrafted you with the ability to give it to others. So not only would you love Him, but you would also be infused with the capacity to love and bond and with the person you enter into a covenant of marriage with, in addition to the bonding with the children the Lord blesses you with.

The problem is that the premature gluing gives birth to false intimacy that fabricates itself as love and this chemical imbalance begins to separate you from God instead of bonding you to Him and the bleeding begins. And when you do like I did, you get the same results. I allowed layers to form on top of one another. I didn't give God permission to go in and uncover them. I just dealt with what was on the surface. I thought I was running from the pain; I was running toward it, not knowing I was becoming more dependent on men and sex than God. The more I buried myself in the layers, the more dependent I became. I'm here to tell you though, you don't have to bleed to death, if you will only give God permission to heal your wound and your broken heart. The same is true here, if you do like I did, you'll get the same results. Thousands of people read this book, see me on TV, look at my life in awe and think that I have some secret to living sexually pure, some big secret to being healed, delivered and made whole. Well, I do. And I'm about to reveal it to you and the rest of the world: I cried…

    Yeah, that's it, that's the big secret of how I received my healing. Cry. I cried out to the Lord like never before and I mean, I cried. Not doing some church dance in the middle of the aisle or 12-step program with twenty people in a group, no, I cried out to the Lord to save me, heal me and deliver me. I received my deliverance in the floor. In the floor with withdrawal symptoms, allowing the Lord to take it out of me. All the residue, the scaring on my spirit, and the pain in my heart. The contamination, the fingerprints, the images in my head, the spirits left on the walls of my cervix, erasing what I came to know as "pleasure", removing the desire and obsession for thrills that caused the bleeding, putting an end to my addiction to 'sexual highs', stripping away every craving and every psychologically dependency, healing my emotions and the chemicals in my brain so that I could learn to love Him, again. Yes, I cried. I cried and I cried and I cried. And I'm here to tell you, there's healing in liquid stitches…..

Psalms 30:2
"O Lord my God, I cried to You and You have healed me."
(Amplified)

Psalms 32:3,5,7
"When I kept silence [before I confessed], my bones wasted away through my groaning all the day long…I acknowledged my sin to You, and my iniquity I did not hide. I said, I will confess my transgressions to the Lord [continually unfolding the past till all is told]-then You [instantly] forgave me the guilt and iniquity of my sin…You are a hiding place for me; You, Lord preserve me from trouble, You surround me with songs and shouts of deliverance. Selah [pause, and calmly think of that]! (Amplified)

Psalms 116:1-8:
"I Love the Lord, because He has heard [and now hears] my voice and my supplications. Because He has inclined His ear to me, therefore will I call upon Him as long as I live. The cords and sorrows of death were around me, and the terrors of Sheol (the place of the dead) had laid hold of me; I suffered anguish and grief (trouble and sorrow). Then called I upon the name of the Lord: O Lord, I beseech You, save my life and deliver me! Gracious is the Lord, and [rigidly] righteous; yes, our God is merciful. The Lord preserves the simple; I was brought low, and He helped and saved me. Return to your rest, O my soul, for the Lord has dealt bountifully with you. For You have delivered my life from death, my eyes from tears, and my feet from stumbling and falling." (Amplified)

    There was nothing I could do or really say that could convey what my heart wanted to reveal to Him. I couldn't think of a word to express my sincerity of the desire that I had to finally be free and to live for Him wholeheartedly, but somehow the tears contained the words. Sometimes I could only fix my lips to say just one word, and since it would be the only words I could finally speak, I chose, Jesus. When I struggled, I called on His name. When I had withdrawals, I cried out His Name. When I was tempted to go back to a life of sin, I cried out His name, Jesus!!!! Only He could understand and interpret what was in my cry for Him. He looked beyond the layers to see what was really in my heart and then He saw sincere worship in my tears. I realized, experienced for myself, that Jesus looked beyond the fact that I was a whore, just like the harlot in Luke 7:36-38.

"He (Jesus) went to the Pharisee's house and sat down at the dinner table. Just then a woman of the village, the town harlot, having learned that Jesus was a guest in the home of the Pharisee, came with a bottle of very expensive perfume and stood at his feet, weeping, raining tears on his feet. Letting down her hair, she dried his feet, kissed them, and anointed them with the perfume." (The Message)

The Pharisee who had invited Jesus was appalled with the fact that Jesus allowed this to happen. He said to himself, "If this Man was the prophet I thought he was, He would have known what kind of woman this is who is falling all over him." Jesus reading his thoughts, posed this question.

"Two men were in debt to a banker. One owed five hundred silver pieces, the other fifty. Neither of them could pay up, and so the banker canceled both debts. Which of the two would be more grateful?"

Simon answered, "I suppose the one who was forgiven the most."

"That's right," said Jesus. Then turning to the woman, but speaking to Simon, He said, "Do you see this woman...She was forgiven many, many sins, and so she is very, very grateful. If the forgiveness is minimal, the gratitude is minimal." Then he spoke to her: "I forgive your sins...Your faith has saved you. Go in peace." Luke 7:41-48 (The Message)

      I don't know about you, but I couldn't pay the debt that I owed, but I was like this harlot, willing to lay my life down to worship Him. I said Lord, "I can't begin to pay you back, I'll never earn enough to compensate you, but I'm willing to love you with my life of worship. I'll do whatever, even if it'll cost me my life." Like this forgiven harlot I was willing to give my greatest possession. The NKJV says that "her sins, which are many, are forgiven, for she loved much." I was ready to love the Lord with all of me, with everything I had. Jesus didn't have to do another thing for me, my sins couldn't be numbered; yet He forgave them all. But even after that, Jesus kept me on His mind, every time He thought about me, He blessed me. I was always on His mind. That's because He remembers worship.

"You can be sure that wherever in the whole world the Message is preached, what she has just done is going to be remembered and admired." Matthew 26:13 (The Message)

If you have only two little sins, then perhaps this may be not for you. But I want to talk to you who have many sins; the one who is still bleeding, even after you've received salvation. You may be hemorrhaging and in pain on the inside, putting off your healing because of the withdrawals but you need to understand that you are running to the pain and away from your healing, turn around and go the other way! You are one floor experience away from receiving your healing! In fact, this is the hour to receive your deliverance. Do you believe that He can do it? If so, then I attach my faith with yours and I declared it done by the authority of Jesus! I break the spirit of bondage off of you, I command satan to dismantle his hold on you, NOW! I speak God's divine healing in your mind, body, and spirit in the name of Jesus! If you are ready to receive your healing, then put this book down, go before the Lord, cry out to Him and grab a hold of your healing!

Finding Mr. Right

"Do two people walk hand in hand if they aren't going to the same place?" Amos 3:3 The Message

As you come to the place of walking in the full manifestation of inner healing, without doubt, many of you will have questions about the proper way of dating as a Christians. Dating is big question mark and has created a lot of controversy among single believers. Many question if they should date, how they should date, or when the right time is for dating. Well, let me ask you this: why do you date? What's your main reason for dating?

Some of you probably answered, "Because I desire a husband/wife." Perhaps, some of you are not ready for marriage and use dating for fun, for leisure, for pass-by time, in the meantime, or in-between time. It's something to do and you just might be lucky—the person you're dating may turn out to be the "one." Many of you date to alleviate loneliness or for security and comfort. Many of you believe that being single automatically gives you the license to date.

In all probability, those of you who date for leisure believe that there is no harm in casual dating. You just loosely do it with no consideration behind it at all. This young lady named Brenda was asked by a man at her church to go out on a date with him and the word "yes" came out of Brenda's mouth without thinking about it. I asked her to tell me his approach and her response in detail. With excitement Brenda told me, "He's so cute and he's an usher at my church. Ty, I bumped into him in the parking lot after church. He told me that he had seen me a couple times, how attractive I was, and asked could he take me out. He's coming to my house on Friday to pick me up for a movie and dinner." A red flag went up because she didn't know this man and he's coming to her house. Concerned, I told Brenda how she should reconsider letting him come to her house and also putt off going out on a date with him with just a two-minute conversation with him in the church parking lot. Uneasy, I said, "Brenda, you should observe him some more, get another opportunity to talk with him to find out a little more about him, perhaps over the phone. If not that, at least drive yourself and meet him at a public place." I came to the conclusion that Brenda didn't like that advice and it just went in one ear and out the other one. She was more excited about the fact that she was going out on a date than *knowing* about this stranger who she was giving access into her life.

Just because a man carries a Bible does not mean that he lives the Bible. What seems to be harmless on the surface could have some hidden dangers beneath it. This is why it is important to observe a person as much as you can before you agree to spending time with them. Sure enough, Brenda called me crying after they went out on their date. This man had not called her after the date and she barely saw him in church and when she did see him in passing, he ignored her and never spoke a hello or any other words to her. I had questions, did the date go sour or you two simply didn't match well? "No, that wasn't the problem at all, Brenda said, "We had a good time. In fact, we went out the next night for another date. At the end of the second date, when we got to my house, he asked if he could come in. We watched a little TV and we started kissing. The kissing led to heavy petting and I stopped him."

It is evident that this man didn't want to have anything to do with Brenda because she wouldn't give him sexual favors. This could have been prevented if Brenda would not have been anxious for "manly company", but instead, she should have sought the Lord concerning this man before going out on a date with him, even asking her pastor or another leader in her church about him and also patiently observe and monitor his lifestyle. Some women, even in the church, are so desperate to get a man or a "bill provider" that they'll do anything to get one. Women are good at fixing up on the outside. But if they are torn up on the inside they can be cunning and sneaky, too. Many of you start dating and you become MIA: missing in action. We won't see you in church because the first thing you'll do is put God on the back burner. This is why the healing process is fundamental before you even consider dating.

I have a friend who is dating this guy who she has "questions" about. To protect the names of the "innocent," we'll call her Lisa. I don't know about Lisa being innocent in this but let's look at her situation. Lisa has been out on a few dates with this guy over the last two months. On the surface, he appears to be a good guy: excellent job, a member of an outstanding church. He opens doors for her, has sent flowers to her workplace (awwhh), and on a couple of occasions, he's cooked gourmet meals for her, **at his house.** One night, he prepared grilled salmon and freshly made fried corn, and they nestled up on the floor to dine and engage in warm conversation. It's interesting to me how you can be so saved . . . until you start dating. Then, your morals, your standards, your love for God is now negotiable.

After this well-served meal, they continue to talk . . . while he's massaging her feet! Now in dreamland, Lisa lays her head back on the couch, her eyes closed in ecstasy. With a raspy voice, he says, "What are doing to me?" Acting clueless, Lisa responds, "Doing what to you?" With equal enjoyment of his foot massage, he answers, "I'm massaging the feet of a beautiful woman whom I have never even had the pleasure of kissing."

If it weren't for the fact that we were in a crowded restaurant while she was telling me this story, I would have flipped the table over. With enough evidence to convict her, I chose to sit there in shock, with my mouth extended open, instead of destroying this beautifully decorated café. Guess what Lisa is doing all this time? Laughing!

"You are a trip, Lisa. You know you are wrong, girl. First off, you are leading this man on. Second, while you are playing with this man, you are setting yourself up to give up the goods. You know right now whether you should or should not continue seeing this guy, but you enjoy the chase. You enjoy the toe rubs, the tulips, and the grilled salmon, while you hold and dangle your womanhood and pretty face over this man's head. All the while you are bonding with him and he's playing right along with you. He does not mind feeding your needs; he'll do whatever it takes to get under your dress. Giving you a few flowers and free meals, in exchange for the goods, actually pans out to be more favorable for him. A couple more romantic nights at this man's house, and oops, his hands are in the candy jar." Not only do you put yourself in a dangerous position, but you also set yourself up for a fall when you endeavor in worldly dating practices.

"I have just started reading your book and I am already being blessed and being set free by it. I want to please God in all that I do. I am a minister at my church teaching the word and leading the youth ministry. My fiancé is a minister also. We both truly love God and have done things to change areas in our relationship where we fall short. We are no longer sexually active.... but we still sometimes spend the night at each others' place. Many times we are watching movies, or reading the word, or just having fun. Is this inappropriate? Are we disappointing God? My heart is hurting because even when we were active, we both were so convicted we prayed and cried in the middle of it.... somehow we ended up going back. This time I don't want us to go back - I can't. I want to be delivered totally. My body is going through withdrawals just wanting to be touched. I didn't know I was so addicted. It's been a while since we have done anything, and I want us to make it to marriage being celibate. Please tell me what to do. Should we not spend as much time together?" E. B. (see response in the Q & A section on the website)

Many single people in the church think that they can do the same things they did when they were out in the world but those rules or games don't apply here. Those worldly dating games you play have consequences you seem to overlook. **Casual dating creates casualty.** Casual dating is an accident waiting to happen. You cannot spend your time with any and everybody and think that it will not have a direct effect on your life. "But we're just friends" is a poor excuse for what's really going on between you. Let me point out a few things to you about the casualty in dating. Just because you choose not to commit yourself in a relationship with someone does not mean that you are not obligating yourself to them. When you casually get involved with or date someone, you are forming a bond, an emotional attachment to them.

> **"Above all else, guard your heart, it affects everything you do."**
> Proverbs 4:23 NCV

The King James Version says that out of the heart flows the issues of life. The devil would like nothing more than to get in your life. Your heart contains the source of your life. Even though a casual relationship may have little significance to you, it is attaching itself to your existence.

> **"A broken heart crushes the spirit."** Proverbs 15:13b NLT

Have you ever seen anyone heartbroken? Have you ever been heartbroken? You can't eat, you can't sleep; you are in anguish. Not only is your heart broken, your life is broken. What happened to your heart had a direct effect on your life.

"Keep vigilant watch over your heart; that's where life starts."
The Message

Even when you casually date, even if you think that you are "just friends", you are bonding, attaching, and tying that person to your life. And just like Lisa, many of you will continue to spend time with someone whom you know is not even marriage material, because of the glue that binds you.

Now, for whatever reason, a relationship has ended and you begin dating someone else, or, for some of you, simultaneously dating a few people. Then, the adhesive is applied to these relationships. Even if you don't sleep with them, they are tied to your emotions. If it doesn't work out or you get tired of them then you move on to the next relationship. The cycle has repeated itself, continuously, and now you have gone through the training grounds for divorce. Yes, your casual dating has trained you to be a professional divorcee. This one didn't work out, so get another one. My spiritual father Dr. Myles Munroe often says that the minute you commit yourself to someone else, then anything that happens to break up that relationship is an emotional divorce.

The reason why it didn't work is because you kept comparing them to all the other relationships you were in. The glue that bonded you with Michael has you comparing him to Brandon, or Joe. You say, "He didn't 'perform' like Tony did. He didn't hold me the right way and he wasn't as good." Now, when God sends you your spouse, you don't have the ability, tenacity, or stick-to-it-ness because of the training ground of casual dating. This is one reason why you cannot just jump into a relationship with someone—because you end up competing with past failures. This is also why you have troubled marriages and high divorce rates: people go right into the marriage with a lot of baggage. The residue from previous relationships is brought right into the marriage. You have not had a chance to heal, but, here you are, making a life-long commitment. Then, you expect the person you are with to repair the damages. But that's not their job.
If you have been using dating to satisfy your fleshly needs, you've created the opportunity for you to have intimacy without commitment. You want sex, but you don't want to make the necessary rightful, commitment (marriage). We have this try-it-before-you-buy-it mentality: I need to see if it's going to satisfy me before I make a commitment. I had a co-worker tell me that he refuses to spend twenty years with a woman who could not

fulfill his sexual needs. This was his justification for having sex before marriage.

Do you want to know what my response was to him? "You are a coward! That lame excuse you have to indulge in sexual sin does not make you exempt. If that's the case, we all can use that excuse. Not only is that a weak excuse for you to have sex, but you have absolutely no trust in God. You don't trust that God can accurately guide you in making a decision as to who you should spend the rest of your life with. God is not confused or lost-you are. You've dated so many women that you don't even see the possibility of being with someone longer than six months. You are just going around sampling, having a taste test of everything. Your dating criteria is based on a big butt and a smile. You don't want a commitment, you want sex. Sex should not be the basis for marrying a woman, anyway! Besides, what if it's the other way around, what if you can't satisfy her, Casanova!"

I realize that an active sex life or casual dating is a cover-up or evidence that there are some other issues that are under the cover. This is where cheap thrill number three comes in: your dependency on people. You feel that another person can give you something that you need. Instead of fulfillment, emptiness settles in. Consequently, cheap-thrilled relationships are formed because one's identity and self-worth cannot be found in other people. Ladies, we are especially good with this. The mentality is that if you do not have a man in your life, then, something is wrong with you. You need him to pay your bills, to whisper in your ear and feed your emotional needs, to tell you how good you look and how much he needs you . . . the validation of a man, the comfort of a man.

To have a man ringing your doorbell, to take you out on dates, gives the appearance that you are secure and complete. That's not security. A door swings on hinges, he's in one minute, and out the next. You are codependent on each other; you feed his manly ego and pride, he feeds your self-esteem and emotional needs. Ladies, it's nothing worse than a man who needs to exhibit and parade his self-worth, or to prove that he's a man. He is in search of his identity. The source of his gratification and the proof that he's a man is displayed in your bed and in that other girl's bed. His identity was formed by a world that told him that his manhood is evident by the number of women he sleeps with. As a result, he's carrying Spiritually Transmitted Diseases (STD).

He walks up to you with twenty-three other women alongside him and introduces himself, "Hi, my name is Mike and I'd like to get to know you [I and 23 other spirits, and also, the spirits they've picked up]." Some of you ladies think that because he's in church, he has been cured of his diseases and infections. Think again. He lacks self-control, decency, and morality. His pride and ego gets in the way of his judgment because he has not surrendered and humbled himself to God. He has refused, ignored, and denied God's power to deliver him. Ladies, again, take note: the Bible speaks about this brand of man in II Timothy 3:3-6.

> They will be unloving and unforgiving; they will slander others and have no self-control; they will be cruel and have no interest in what is good. They will betray their friends, be reckless, be puffed up with pride, and love pleasure rather than God. They will **act** as if they are religious, but they will reject the power that could make them godly. **You must stay away from people like that.** They are the kind who work their way into people's homes and win the confidence (take captive) of vulnerable women who are burdened down with the guilt of sin and controlled by many desires. NLT

Caution signs need to be positioned carefully because satan is a manipulator who loves to fabricate the truth. Carbon copies come in all shapes and sizes. You do know what a carbon copy is, don't you? It was just described to you: he's the kind of man that looks and acts just like the man you prayed for. He attends church, buys you flowers and whispers the "I love you's" in your ear, wears a freshly pressed crease in his pants, quote Scriptures, prays over his meal before eating—but is a stranger to

God. I don't know anything worse than a man who does not live his life for God. He couldn't possibly love you; he does not know how to.

The Message translation in this same text refers to women who are taken captive by such men as unstable and needy. Listen up, brothers, there's nothing worse than a needy woman. The criteria for being with this kind of woman does not come cheap. There are excessive obligations attached because you are required to meet the emotional needs and the stability that she lacks. Remember, she has been tampered with by previous relationships and because she lacks self-worth, she needs you to define it for her. Her past is probably filled with men who've disappointed her, or left her to be a single parent, so she's not only resentful but confused as to whether she should submit to you or she maintain her independence. *"Are you like the others? Are you going to stay or are you going to go? Can I trust you? Is my hair pretty? He must be cheating, I don't trust him. Why hasn't he called me? I'm gaining weight. Maybe I should change my hair color. Why hasn't he told me that he loves me? Is he my husband?"* . . . I know she's pretty and her Bible has her name engraved on it, but did you check for the warning label? DO NOT USE IF SEAL HAS BEEN TAMPERED!

The Bible tells us in I Corinthians 6:19 that your life as a single Christian is protected and sealed by the Holy Spirit. That seal guarantees purity and guards you from contamination. Fraudulent relationships that have developed from casual dating and sexual relationships will tamper with the seal and open the door for defilement. Not only are you needy, but unstable:

> A man of two minds is unstable and unreliable and uncertain about everything he thinks, feels and decides. James 1:8 Amplified

The problem, again, reverts back to compromising your faith and wavering back and forth between two opinions. A double-minded person lives a double life. There is no way that you can live your life based on God's standards one day, then choose to date the way you did when you lived for the devil. The inconsistency or lack of commitment to serve God whole-heartedly allows the enemy to set you up. It goes on to say in II Timothy 3:6, 7 that not only can you not think for yourself, but you can't feel or make decisions apart from a man.

"For among them are those who worm their way into homes and captivate silly and weak-natured and spiritually dwarfed women, loaded down with [the burden of their] sins [and easily] swayed and led away by various evil desires and seductive impulses. [These weak women will listen to anybody who will teach them]; they are forever inquiring and getting information, but are never able to arrive at a recognition and knowledge of the Truth." Amplified

When you are spiritually dwarfed, your growth has been stunted and you continue to fall prey to evil desires (sexual urges and cravings, fornication, sexual immorality) and seductive impulses (one-night stands and three-week relationships). This is what I call the "treadmill syndrome"; going back and forth to church every week but giving no evidence of change. You stay the same way: lacking control, no restraints, vulnerable, wounded, needy, with low self-esteem, weak-minded, and naïve. You continue to live in your past and never move forward. Take a look at your last three to five relationships. More than likely, they mirror or replicate one another. They form a continued cycle of repeating your past. How do you end this vicious cycle? Rid yourself of your opinion on dating and discontinue the use of advice from other people who are spiritually uneducated. You will never arrive at the truth. Replace your opinion with God's opinion.

Let's look at some worldly dating traditions that are contrary to the Word of God, like kissing. An overwhelming number of you believe that it is okay to kiss open-mouthed. Let me ask you this, why do you kiss? For pleasure. It stimulates you; you get sexual arousal from "tongue kissing." Open-mouth kissing is sexual in its nature and it's actually a way of "having sex" without actually having sex. It serves a fleshly need; it is foreplay. Let me remind you that foreplay is sexual stimulation intended as a prelude to sexual intercourse.

There were a number of people who followed Jesus, who knew the law: not to murder, not to kill, not to commit adultery, and so on and so forth. It's funny, though, because Jesus always found Himself having to define the law in-depth. Some of these folks thought that if they didn't actually take a knife and kill someone, then, they didn't commit murder. But throughout the Bible, you can find that gossip and slander can cut someone just like a knife could. Hence, you have people who have not necessarily made reservations at a hotel room to sleep with their lovers, but who would sit and fantasize, daydream and lust about an affair, or picture themselves performing sexual acts with a lover. Matthew 5:27, 28 tells us:

> You have heard that the law of Moses says, "Do not commit adultery." But I say, anyone who even looks at a woman with lust in his eye has already committed adultery with her in his heart. NLT

So, like Jesus, I have to spell it out for some of you who think that mouth/tongue kissing is okay to do. Jesus said that if you **look** at a woman in lust, you've committed adultery. How much more if you actually touch or tongue-strangle them? If the very thought of lusting after someone is considered adultery/fornication, then, quite naturally, kissing would be fornication. The Bible also says that you should greet one another with a holy kiss.[8] If you don't feel holy, but get goose bumps up and down your spine, get aroused, and are prompted to perform other sexual acts, then, that kiss is not holy! Let's read more about this in James 3:5-10:

> So also, the tongue is a small thing, but what enormous damage it can do. A tiny spark can set a great forest on fire. And the tongue is a flame of fire. It is full of wickedness that can ruin your whole life. It can turn the

entire course of your life into a blazing flame of destruction, for it is set on fire by hell itself. People can tame all kinds of animals and birds and reptiles and fish, but no one can tame the tongue. It is an uncontrollable evil, full of deadly poison. Sometimes it praises our Lord and Father, and sometimes it breaks out into curses against those who have been made in the image of God. And so blessing and cursing come pouring out of the same mouth. Surely, my brothers and sisters, this is not right! NLT

You can't kiss someone in the mouth, get stimulation from it, and then control it; you are flirting with sensual passion. I guarantee you that it is building you up to perform other sexual pleasures. You only need one spark and it'll set your whole body on fire. The tongue is untamable. You start kissing then heavy petting and touching follows. Yet this is the same tongue with which you worship God! This is the same mouth you speak in tongues with, but then, you put your tongue in the mouth of someone you are not married to. Surely, my brothers and sisters, this is not right.

If anyone considers himself religious and yet does not keep a tight rein on his tongue, he deceives himself and his religion is worthless. James 1:26 NLT

Another worldly dating concept is contraceptives. Throw away the condoms and birth control pills! You can't successfully overcome lust with a failure plan. When you carry condoms in your wallet, your mind is made up to have sex. Don't give me that "just in case" statement or say that this is safe sex. Even if the condom prevents a disease or a pregnancy, it still does not protect you from sin and its consequences. The only safe sex is celibacy. Not having sex at all until you get married is not only safe sex, but it is also birth control, protection, disease and sin control. You do not need a back-up plan like condoms and birth control pills when you believe that God has equipped you with the power to refrain from sex until you get married.

You might have heard of the expression, "Why would you buy the whole cow, when you already get the milk and beef for free?" I know he has told you he is going to marry you, but why would he, when he already has you there in the house, ironing his clothes, serving dinner on the table every night, and do I have to mention that the "candy store" is always open? He has no incentive now, because you have given him the rewards of commitment without charge. "Shacking up"—living with a man or a woman you are not married to—is satan's idea, not God's. The house, the shack that you two live in, could be a mansion, but if you are not married, it is built on a foundation that's subject to collapse. Anything that's not built on the foundation or the principles of God is a shack and can do only one thing: shackle you. It will chain your thoughts and your actions.

Stacey, who has been in a relationship with Jerry for more than 20 years, is waiting around for Jerry to marry her. She has pleaded with him and has even given him ultimatums, yet, he has not married her. Stacey has told Jerry that she is going to leave in 3 weeks if he doesn't marry her. Three weeks pass, Stacey is still there and Jerry still has not asked to marry her. Another demand comes from Stacey after times goes by and no proposal. Guess what? He's not going to marry her. It's been 20 years. Jerry knows that she is not going anywhere. She has threatened him many times, putting her bags at the door, but never fulfilling the promise of leaving. Though Stacey constantly has to wonder where he is at two o'clock in the morning if he's not lying next to her. How can she leave? Stacey is chained to her thoughts, her actions and to this relationship. Talk about a prisoner of love! But don't think the situation is any different if you've only been shacking up with someone for a year. Her shackles started out as a year too. . . . Now its twenty years later and she is still chained.

The Bible declares in Genesis 2:24 that "A man leaves his mother, to cleave to his wife." God is faithful and loyal to you. When you entrusted your life to God, He made you a promise in Hebrews 13:5, "I'll never leave you, nor forsake you." He would send you someone who is the same—one who firmly takes on the role of a provider, protector, companion, etc. He would be dependable and trustworthy. If he does not mirror God, he is a fraud. You cannot trust a man who will not dedicate himself to God or to you; he can always take flight. If he does not marry you, if he does not cleave, he can always leave.

Dating someone you have nothing in common with is another issue. I'm not talking about the fact that he likes Western movies and you like comedy. I'm referring to the fact that he is an uncircumcised Philistine, a God-hater who has no knowledge of the Truth, carrying out satan's will, while you have declared Jesus as Lord. Let me really break this down for you. He or she is the type that has no desire to go to church, and when you bring it up, you two get into an argument. She is one that always prompts you to compromise your belief, especially when it comes to sleeping with you. Brothers, the Bible warns you about this kind of woman in Proverbs 23:27-28:

> A whore is a bottomless pit; a loose woman can get you in deep trouble fast. She'll take you for all you've got; she's worse than a pack of thieves. The Message

Of course, she is not the type to stand on the corner; satan is more cunning than that. She is an undercover whore in disguise. Everything about her seems to be good, but if he or she is not living for Jesus, I don't care how nice she is, you are dating satan. If she has no regard for godly principles and is not interested in living them, again, she could be the most perfect person in every other area, but if she's missing the main ingredient, Jesus, the relationship is void, worthless, and has no value whatsoever.

Ladies, how often have you said, "I'm going to get him 'saved.' I'm going to lead him to the Lord." How do you suppose you will do that? You didn't save yourself. Besides, he does not hear a word you are saying when you are lying next to him in bed with no clothes on. The next time you hear someone say they're going to save someone by living with them, or having sex with them, have them read II Corinthians 6:14.

"Do not be unequally yoked with unbelievers [do not make mismated alliances with them or come under a different yoke with them, inconsistent with your faith]. For what partnership have right living and right standing with God with iniquity and lawlessness? Or how can light have fellowship with darkness?" Amplified

"But you don't understand, Ty, I love him." I have heard this so many times, and I do understand. That "but" is a compromise and you are in negotiation with satan and you are giving him permission to contaminate you. A yoke is a bow-shaped bar used for joining a pair of animals at the neck. It's used to get them to work in unison, to work together. When you are in a relationship with a man who does not operate in the principles of God, who is an enemy to God (and that's what he is if he is not saved), you have this bar around your neck, yoking you two together. You will not be able to agree because he does not believe what you believe. He does not go to church, he's going out to the bar, drinking, lying and cheating, cursing, buying bootleg videotapes, going to the casino, and trying to put his hands in your panties. He's living a life of hell, while you are trying to keep your life holy. That's a holy hell!

I was in your position. I was seeing this guy who I considered to be the "perfect package." He was extremely attentive to my every need, cooked gourmet meals, was supportive, had no baggage from previous relationships, was compassionate, financially stable (not employed but the owner of the company), faithful, and he loved me. He was calculating me into his 401k and retirement plans. We were advancing towards marriage. The one problem was: he was not saved. Oh, he went to church, he was ethical, he had the Donnie McClurkin collection—all types of gospel music. He "knew of" Jesus, but he didn't *live* for him. I was hurt and angry. "A good man gone to waste."

Instead of leaving, I wanted to stay and get him "saved." You know, evangelistic dating. I loved him . . . It was hard to let him go. I thought he was the one who was compromising. The Lord set the record straight, "No, Ty, you are the one who's compromising." As much a he was a good, well-packaged man . . . it didn't mean anything. Life outside of Christ is, simply, death, and I wasn't willing to have a good man in place of Jesus.

Let's look at this same text of Scripture again in The Message translation. I need to clarify some other things.

Don't become partners with those who reject God. How can you make a partnership out of right and wrong? That's not partnership; that's war. Is light best friends with dark? Does Christ go strolling with the Devil? Do trust and mistrust hold hands? Who would think of setting up pagan idols in God's holy Temple? But that is exactly what we are, each of us a temple in whom God lives…So leave the corruption and compromise; leave it for good, says God. Don't link up with those who will pollute you.

You can be unequally yoked with a believer. My friend, Minister Limara, said to me one day that about seventy-five percent of the PRADA or COACH bags or purses you see in beauty supply stores, boutiques or on the streets are not real. She said, "Ty, you buy one of those fake purses and you could never go inside a COACH store and take advantage of the privilege of replacing a broken strap. They'll detect that it's a fake in a minute."

My point is, there's a lot of good-looking believers who are faking and compromising it. Just about everybody is so-called "saved" now. The Amplified Bible said do not become unequally yoked with unbelievers, those inconsistent with your faith. There are "believers" who only live certain parts of the Bible, go to church, pray or read the Word when they feel like it, drink, curse, sleep around and live inconsistently with their faith. Just because they're believers does not mean you can spend time with them or date them. They're believers, but what do they <u>believe</u>? The proof or evidence is in how they live. Don't tell me that they're ministers. I've witnessed ministers who sleep around, get ushers in the church pregnant and still preach a good sermon. Go beyond the title. They'll do and live what they truly believe.

While I'm on the subject, **it means nothing to God that you will not date a sinner, but you'll date a believer and sin.** Just because you won't go out or spend time with a man or a woman who lives a sinful lifestyle, has not accepted Jesus as his or her Lord, and lives a sinful lifestyle does not mean anything if you are sleeping with, shacking up, kissing or lusting with a person who has accepted Jesus. Tell me, what's the difference?

There's something I call "Egypt" mentality. Here you are, set free by the power of God, but still dependent on "baby's daddy." Okay, it was a "mistake", a bad judgment call. But why do you continue to allow him to come over and sleep with you in exchange for diapers, light bill money, and car note? Do you realize that it's his responsibility to buy his child diapers, clothes, food . . . to provide the needs for his child . . . by all means, the bare necessities? The Bible says in I Timothy 5:8 that a man who does not take care of his child is worse than an infidel, an unbeliever. An unbeliever's fate is eternal death in hell. Can you imagine anything worse than that? Well, that's the fate of a man who will not even take care of his own child.

Look at the millions of dollars owed in child support. God is so passionate about this because it's the essence of who He is. He is a father and He would never abandon His children or not take care of them. The Bible says in Luke 12:22 and 23 that it's not only His responsibility, but it's His pleasure. He would never manipulate you, especially for goods, in place of something He's responsible for. And for a man to do that to his child's mother is appalling! You would never deny your child clothes, neglect to feed him or take care of him, or go and visit the baby just because his father won't sleep with you. Such actions are worthy of eternal death.

Fathers, don't blame the baby. You wouldn't have had that child if **you** didn't have sex. Don't let your baby suffer the consequences because of your irresponsibility. Reverse the judgment of eternal death. Repent, get responsible for your actions, and take care of your child. God will not only restore unto you eternal life, but He will restore your relationship with your child and show you how to become a father, a daddy . . . just like Him. Now, back to you, my sista. You murmur and complain because you have to trust God to pay the bills. It's easier to give up a li'l of yourself, in exchange for a new pair of shoes. This is especially not good if he's not your child's father. I know someone who has a nine-year-old son and a fourteen-year-old girl whom she allows to see her heavy casual-dating lifestyle. She allows a few of her male acquaintances to come over to her house for "visits." She is teaching her son that this is what men do—run up in and out of a woman's house without a commitment. She's training her daughter how to run drive-thru relationships and that it's okay to give up a little to get a little. Kids do not do what you say, they do what you do.

    I know quite a number of people who have "exchange" relationships with someone because of what they can provide. Most of them are afraid to let the relationship go because they don't believe that they can survive without their "partners". They simply don't trust God to provide their every need. I had one girl call me with heaviness in her voice, "Ty, I know I need to let him go but I don't know how I'm going to pay my car note. Some of my bills are in his name, like my cell phone bill. He pays for my hair to get done . . ." She just went on and on until I stopped her, "You call me every week, saying you are going to leave him, every time you come from church. If you really are sincere and really want to please God, then, you would go without a cell phone."

    She interrupted me, "But you don't understand . . ." I knew that common statement was coming. I stopped her with, "Don't tell me I don't understand. You are making your decision clear as to where your loyalty is. Either you love God and live for Him, or the convenience of having mobile communication is greater. Can you hear me now? But if you truly love God, then you would leave that meaningless relationship, even if it means that you pull your hair to the back and wear a pony tail for six months, catch the bus to work, and move back home with momma."

The first thing that someone in this situation will try to tell me is that I don't understand. But trust me, I do. I've been in just about every situation in relationships that you can think of. Here's an example: I had just moved into an apartment, with no job. I spent my last money on the deposit and the first month's rent. Everyday, I would tell the Lord, "You are my Daddy and I trust You." I was so broke, it was ridiculous. I was looking for work, but a week would go by and there was no call, no sign of money or work. It was getting closer and closer to rent time and the refrigerator still had an echo in it. Then one day the phone rang. It was someone I'll call Deon who I knew in the entertainment industry and he said, "Ty, I want you to do me a favor. I know at one time I wanted you to be my wife but you never gave a brotha' a chance. But I just want you to do me a favor."

"Okay, you are beating around the bush. What kind of favor?" I was suspicious. You know, you can get that way when someone starts out with "I need a favor." He finally answered, "I don't want you to be my girlfriend or my 'baby's mamma.' I don't want you to be my wife, I don't even want you to sleep with me. Just do me one favor. Let me pay your bills." Broke as I was, that sounded like "amazing grace how sweet the sound" to my ears. With a smile on my face, I said, "You know what, I thank you so much for thinking about me and my needs, but I'm okay. I'm well taken care of. Just do me a favor . . . Pray for me."

I hung up the phone, swallowed the lump in my throat, and thought about pleading with God to let me call him back. Instead, I said, "Daddy, you are my provider. I have never seen the righteous forsaken, nor his seed begging for bread. I am like Abraham in Genesis 14:22 and 23, I will not let another man put a shoelace on these shoes. Until You send me my husband, You are just going to have to pay the rent, get my hair and nails done, feed and clothe me." See, even though Deon was a man in the church, a well-known artist, Bible-totin' and all, I knew it was a set-up. This goes back to knowing yourself—your weaknesses and struggles. My past struggles were relationships and sex, and satan remembered that. I don't care how saved you are, he'll try to come back and trip you up in those areas where you struggle. I would have let this man start paying my bills, and, months later, he would have been in my bed.

Some of my female friends told me that was God trying to bless me. I laughed, "That tells me that you don't know my Daddy, because He will not send a blessing that will have me dependent on a man. He'll send a check in the mail anonymously before He does that." It would have been much easier for me to take Deon's money and no one would have known, except God. I did not use the bills as an excuse; instead, I did what pleased Him. I continued to trust God and you would have thought that God would have showed up immediately. He didn't. You are going to have to live for God, even when things are not going your way, even with shut-off notices and an empty refrigerator. I kept the faith and trusted God beyond the last five cents. I didn't have to sleep with a man to get what I needed; I did it God's way. I trusted Him and He rewarded that trust as He had promised in Hebrews 11:6.

Then, the phone rang again. It was an entertainment company that got a hold of my bio. They wanted to talk with me about coming aboard to do some marketing work for their company. I went in to see them and they offered me double the pay that they usually hire marketing consultants for. I don't care how high your bills are, how low your income is, trust God! Trust God and walk away from that toxic relationship. He will make sure that your needs are met. You don't have to continue to sell yourself. God, your Father, will provide for you. Again, it's God's responsibility and pleasure. You are worth more than a $100 light bill and a $500 car note. It is totally up to you. You can stay in bondage for another forty years or you can seek God's face and receive what He has for you: freedom from sexual sin.

By now you can see why casual dating is a problem. It keeps you in a trap. I have friends who confuse or equate the fact that I don't date with not wanting a man, or that I don't want to get married. That's far from the truth. The truth is, dating often puts you in a position where you constantly compromise, and it can be a distraction that takes you off the path that God has for you. The word "distract" simply means to take or divert one's path, focus, mind, or attention; to trouble greatly in the mind. And the Bible tell us in I Corinthians 7:32, 34-35,

"An unmarried man can spend his time doing the Lord's work and thinking how to please him . . . In the same way, a woman who is no longer married or has never been married can be more devoted to the Lord in body and in spirit . . . I am saying this for your benefit, not to place restrictions on you. I want you to do whatever will help you serve the Lord best, with as few distractions as possible."

Some of you are no doubt asking, "But how can you find Mr. Right if you don't date?" Now, don't get me wrong, dating has its place, but some of you are not equipped or don't know how to date. I believe dating is for the sole purpose of determining if this is someone you should spend the rest of your life with . . . not for practicing marriage. This does not mean that you spend time with everybody who asks you for your phone number. But before you can consider dating properly you must be healed from your past.

You are not ready to be pursued by a man, ladies, nor are you ready to find a wife, brothers, if there has been no inward change, if you have not been healed from your past, and if you have not been renewed by the Word. You cannot recognize a good, godly man or woman if you have not had a metamorphosis, a change, a transformation of yourself. You are not complete until you have allowed God to renew you into your original condition, because you cannot give from an empty cup. You are not only cheating yourself, but the person you are with, because you have nothing to give him or her. Here's what the Bible has to say in Proverbs 30:21, 23 about women who have not allowed the Lord to heal them prior to marriage:

> "There are three things that make the earth tremble. No, four it cannot endure . . . . A bitter woman who finally gets a husband." NLT

There is a red light here: **marriage does not complete you, God does.** You better get yourself together before you say "I do." If you are trying to get into a relationship because you need someone to help pay the bills, or you need someone to hold you or you want to have sex, you are in trouble. Because you are burning with passion, it better not be the reason why you want to get married, because sex will not keep you together. I heard a married woman say that there are more single people having sex than married folks. Isn't that backwards!

Let's look at the statistics. More than half of all first-time marriages end in divorce. Some of you think that the statistics don't affect you because you are a Christian and you go to church. But think again. The divorce rate of the church mirrors that of the world. More than fifty percent of those who are in the church, who proclaim Jesus as Lord, are divorcing, too. This tells me that a lot of folks in the church are getting married without God's consent and you have two people who are not complete in Christ.

We get so preoccupied with getting married that we do not even stop and get the "green light" from God. The reason why people don't get God's permission is because they know it's not a good decision. You want this one to be the "right one" so bad that you'll stay in the relationship, even after you've seen the clear signs that you have to get out of it. My partner Kim says it this way, "If you do not want to become that person, you need to stop seeing them." Look at that person's total life and ask yourself if you are willing to become what that person is. Remember, whatever they have, whatever they are, is what you will have and become. But it's only when the honeymoon is over when we begin to call on God . . . when the wolf takes off the sheep's clothing. One thing I do know is that when God's hand is in it, it's eternal. If you don't have God's approval from the beginning, you'll find yourself crying out for Him in the end. Save yourself the time, the drama and the despair.

Let's look at Genesis 2:18-22 for the first man-and-woman relationship in the Bible.

And the Lord God said, "It is not good for the man to be alone. I will make a companion who will help him." So the Lord God formed from the soil every kind of animal and bird. He brought them to Adam to see what he would call them, and Adams chose a name for each one. He gave names to all the livestock, birds, and wild animals. But still there was no companion suitable for him. So the Lord God caused Adam to fall into a deep sleep. He took one of Adam's ribs and closed up the place from which he had taken it. The Lord God made woman from the rib and brought her to Adam.

There are a couple of points I need to make. First, the Lord said to Adam that it is not good for man to be alone. Instead of immediately giving him a woman, God gave him a job, ladies. Then, God took Adam and put him to sleep. What was the significance of Adam's flesh being put to sleep? It means you should not accept a man whose flesh has not been put to sleep—dead! If the flesh is not crucified, if the flesh is not dead, you will find yourself dealing with someone who is out of control, with no stability, or with no regard for the principles of God.

Another thing to note is that you cannot prepare yourself for a mate and market yourself at the same time. This is the time for developing and committing yourself to Christ, not the time for dating. You cannot commit yourself to a man or a woman when you are not committed to your relationship with God. God did not give Adam a mate until he was prepared and qualified for it. You are praying for someone you don't even qualify for. "Lord, I want a man who is saved, who is spiritual, prays everyday, knows the Bible, well-groomed, cute, works hard, looks after me, who can take care of me . . . in Jesus' name. Amen."

Are you really prepared or qualified for what you are asking for? Would you want to marry someone like you or are you praying for something you are not? Allow God to prepare you, to line you up and then,, *wait* until God presents you to that man, like Eve. The last thing you want is to get antsy and move out of God's timing and order.

I know a woman I'll call Vicky who wanted so badly to be married that she planned and gave herself a bridal shower. She bought herself a dress, with no engagement ring or a man in sight. She called herself operating in faith. That is not faith, it's foolishness! It's foolish to have people show up at your bridal shower when you don't even have someone interested in you. She was so anxious to have a man in her life that she took action (outside of God's order). Soon after this shower, Vicky met a guy and married him. They separated after three months. Trust me, the devil will send you just what you are looking for. Don't get in such a hurry to get married that you make a foolish move.

Like Vicky, you may have made no inward change, but you want a husband. You cannot move or act outside of God's orders and think that it's going to work. You must wait! A friend put it to me this way: "Do you like fruit, Ty? I love fruit! I love apples, plums, bananas, and especially pears. They're so juicy and sweet," he said. He started making me hungry. I pictured some sweet, black cherries. I could almost taste them. Then he said, "I love fruit, but have you ever had a banana when it wasn't ripe or a pear? It's the nastiest thing ever; it leaves a bitter taste in your mouth."

That's exactly what happens when you don't wait on God. You can jump into a relationship with someone and if it is not stamped and approved by God, you'll pull dating off the tree too soon and you'll take a bite into it and it'll leave a bitter, nasty taste in your life. But if you wait for the "ripe" time—God's timing—then, you will enjoy the rewards of a relationship that goes beyond courting and into a forever covenant with someone who truly loves you. Wait on God. Until then, you are in reserve.

Remember, you are special to God. He does not want you to hook up with just anyone. He's not holding you back because He doesn't want you with anyone or for you to be alone the rest of your life. He loves you more than you love yourself. He is keeping you back, holding you in reserve for a special use, a special somebody. You have put yourself and your talents to unworthy use for far too long.

Now some of you don't like the word "waiting", because you don't know the art or beauty of waiting. My good friends Jerome and Alena have been in the restaurant and food industry for years. Jerome said something that I'll never forget, "God's people have used the word 'waiting' incorrectly. They say 'I'm just waiting on the Lord,' but have their hands crossed the whole time. In a restaurant when the wait staff is at your table to serve you, they are not standing there with their arms folded. The waitress walks up to your table, takes your order, and then, he or she will go and get what you've asked for."

This is what you do while you wait on God to send you your husband or wife: you walk right up to the Throne Table and ask, "Lord, may I take your order?" Then you go and fulfill the order. A lot of single people have had it so backwards. Our "waiting season" consists of idle, casual dating instead of "taking orders." While waiting, we date, instead of serving God. Yet, it's clearly written in Psalms 62:5-8,

> God, the one and only--I'll wait as long as he says. Everything I hope for comes from him, so why not? He's solid rock under my feet, breathing room for my soul, An impregnable castle: I'm set for life. My help and glory are in God-granite-strength and safe-harbor-God--So trust Him absolutely, people; lay your lives on the line for Him. God is a safe place to be. The Message

This is why so many single people spend their time dating or searching for someone. They need someone to fill the time. You notice that Adam had to be put to sleep. He was so busy that he didn't know he needed someone. He was on the wait staff for God, taking orders and carrying hem out. God is the one that caused him to recognize that he should not live alone. Adam was too busy to be lonely. I often hear Dr. Mike Murdock, a phenomenal wisdom teacher, say that loneliness is not the absence of affection, but **the absence of direction.** This is why Adam was not lonely: he had direction.

So, the question is, do you know where you are going? Where are you going? If you don't get anything else, get what I'm about to say. You don't need a pass-by time, you don't need someone to hold you, you don't need to lay with some woman, and you don't need a man to take you out for a happy meal or a back rub . . . **You don't need a man to date, you need a MANDATE.** You are not lonely or in need of companionship. **You're going around looking for a thrill, when all you need to do is follow God's will.**

> Then Jesus explained: "My nourishment comes from doing the will of God, who sent me, and from finishing his work. John 2:34 NLT

This is one of the reasons why you and many other single people fall prey to sexual sin and toxic relationships—because you are not taking God's order or mandate. You are devoid of purpose. It's the very reason why God created you, and you either have no idea what it is *or* you know what it is but have not responded to it. The mandate, the assignment, the purpose why God created you is lying dormant, waiting for you. This is why you can live with a man who refuses to make a commitment with you, woman of God . . . why you can't seem to throw that black book away, man of God . . . This is why you can stay in a relationship that is ungodly and unhealthy, because you don't know your purpose . . . You are trespassing.

You remain in situations and places that God never wanted or created for you to be in. You stay in environments and with people that eat away at and kill your existence. When you do not operate in your purpose, you improperly use your talents, abilities, time, and your life . . . with people who've interrupted God's plan for your life. Time spent in search of destiny was wasted in fatal, fraudulent relationships, in people who only pushed you further away from your purpose.

    You don't have any direction because your vision is blurred. You can't see where you are going or where you need to be when your path is blocked with trespassers. Your 20/20 vision is off because casual dating is a distraction. I don't know about you, but I have wasted a lot of time in sin and with people who were decoys to my destiny, and I don't have time to give anymore. I can't waste any more of my time; my time is spent on purpose, not on sin or catastrophic relationships. And, now, you need to end these relationships, immediately, and at all costs. Get yourself right so that the Lord can position you for Mr. Right.

Chapter Nine: The Lover of Your Soul

There are 365 days in a year. There are 8,760 hours and 52 weeks in a year, 168 hours in a week, 24 hours and 1,440 seconds in a day. They say the average lifespan is about 70 years for a human being. This means that you would live 29,200 days, 700,800 hours, and 42,048,000 seconds during your entire life! How much of that time would you spend with God?

Well, let's see. There are only 52 Sundays in a year. On average, a church service will run about 2 hours. Providing that you go to church every Sunday, this would mean that out of 700,800 hours of your life, only 8,320 of those hours would be spent with God. That's about one percent of the time in your life that you give to Him. **In essence, you will live your whole life and come to realize that you've only lived one percent of it.** If your life is nothing without Him, and it is, then, ninety-nine percent of your life would be wasted and lived in vain.

We have used Sunday morning church services as time well spent with God. We live as illegitimate, bastard children by only letting Mother (the church) raise us, as if we have a deadbeat father who's only good for "child support blessings." We've allowed our worldly and tainted habits to spill over into our relationship with the Father. Our one-night stands, short-lived relationships and quickie bedroom lifestyles have permeated and penetrated through the pores of our fellowship with Him. We go on our two-hour date, 52 times out of each year, call it a relationship and think we should get rewarded for it. When it doesn't pay off, we have the audacity to blame God when all hell breaks loose. We don't want to make a commitment with Him, we'll backslide if it won't go our way, and our two-minute prayers are in the words of "Give me, give me, give me."

Backslide? Slide back to what and serve who? No one gets the credit for keeping you from going out of your mind, sticking with you when everybody else turned their backs on you (including the man who promised you the world), healing your body, rescuing you from debt and troubles that you yourself caused, delivering you from depression, forgiving you time after time even when you said you wouldn't again, loving you when you couldn't love yourself, being faithful to you when you weren't, sparing your life from death . . . No one gets the credit, no one . . . it was only Jesus! If it was not for Him, hell would have been your home.

II Corinthians 5:21 declares, "For he hath made him to be sin for us, who knew no sin; that we might be made the righteousness of God in him." Sin prevented you from having the relationship that God longed to have with you. Since the fall of man, God's intent and purpose was to get back and restore the fellowship, the relationship He once had with His children. He was willing to do anything to get that back, even if it meant sacrificing His only Son, Jesus. God cannot look upon sin, because He is a Holy God. Sin placed a wall between you and God, so He had to recreate or redeem you in His image in order to restore the relationship. He needed a spotless, uncontaminated, holy sacrifice and the only person worthy or who could even meet that criteria was Jesus.

Before Jesus, no one was worthy or holy enough to enter into God's presence. In Leviticus 4, the priest in the Old Testament had to go before God for you behind a veil. You couldn't go in. And if the priest didn't have his act together, they'd drag him out dead by a string. Sin could not go in the presence of a Holy God. The Bible tells us in II Corinthians 3:14, the veil that separated man from God was stripped when Jesus' uncontaminated, holy, sacrificial Blood was shed on the Cross. You can now enter into the presence of God without the stench of sin killing you, because of the Blood of Jesus. How dare we not access the honor and privilege of going before the Father!

The religious Pharisees are not about to like what I'm about to say; neither can they understand or conceive the depth of it. But if you would grab a hold of what I'm about to say, you will understand that you don't ever have to be entangled again in sexual immorality. You can no longer use sin as an excuse. The Word of God says that Jesus, who knew no sin, **became sin**. This means that the sins that you committed, Jesus became them, so that you could be made right with God. In order for you to be right with God, somebody had to take on your sins, or you wouldn't be able to stand in His presence. Somebody had to take them, somebody had to take the punishment for your sins, somebody had to die for them . . . Jesus did.

He became every sinful act that you committed, your lust, every time you put your mouth on somebody . . . He became that. Every time you laid down with somebody, He became that—that adulterous relationship you were in, that woman you slept with whom you were not married to, that man you fell on your knees for, the pornography that you watched, the masturbation, the homosexuality, the oral sex . . . He became that. My God, my God, you ought to fall down and worship at the thought of Jesus loving you that much to take on every foul sin that you have committed!

Jesus became death for you, beaten beyond recognition. Isaiah 52:14 says that the crucifixion of Jesus was so brutal that you could not even tell that He was a man because of the overflow of blood that covered his entire body. Seven-inch nails in His hands and feet, a crown of thorns in His head . . . all so that you could stand before God. They sarcastically said to Him, "Save yourself if you are really God's Chosen One." He could have, but if He had gotten up, you would have had to take His place. He stayed until sin was finished. "No one takes my life. I lay it down and I'll pick it back up. I have the power and the authority." John 10:18

You have that same power. You don't have to lay your body down again in sin. You possess the power and the authority to maintain your sexual purity. The marred, bloody image of Jesus on the Cross should remind you that He became your sin and to lie back down in it is only crucifying and putting the nails back in Him again. We read in Hebrews 6:4-6 (NLT):

> "For it is impossible to restore to repentance those who were once enlightened—those who have experienced the good things of heaven and shared in the Holy Spirit, who have tasted the goodness of the word of God and the power of the age to come—and who then turn away from God. It is impossible to bring such people to repentance again because they are nailing the Son of God to the Cross again by rejecting Him, holding Him up to public shame."

A deadly kiss of betrayal is what sent Jesus to the Cross. You will not be another Judas and kiss Jesus on the face while at the same time crucify Him with sexual sin. No, it's time for an "at the point of no return" kind of commitment. "I ain't looking back, I ain't going back. No, you are not going to put your hand on me. No, you can't get a little 'feel,' I don't give my pearls to swine. I am holy and in right standing with God and I will not let sin stand between me and my Daddy."

> "But the time is coming and is already here when true worshipers will worship the Father in spirit and in truth. The Father is looking for anyone who will worship Him that way. For God is Spirit, so those who worship him must worship in spirit and truth." John 4:23-24 (NLT)

It's time for the true worshipers, who are determined to live their lives for Jesus for real. The real worshippers are not sleeping around. There's a big difference between religion and relationship. You can be religious, attend church, and *know* of God and not live holy, but you can't be in a relationship with

Him and not live holy. There's no more fakin' it. True worshippers have a relationship and they *know* all about the One they serve. The Father is looking for anyone who will worship Him that way, to be in a relationship with Him, to know Him.

Worship is a lifestyle, a lifestyle of holy living, reflecting the image of God daily. True worship is not just proclaiming it, but living it. True worship is where the two-minute prayers for getting blessings go to a lying-in-a-prostrate position for intimacy. True worship is when the relationship goes from Sunday morning worship to private long talks in the Secret Place. Where the relationship goes from mental assent of "I know that God saved me" to "I know You are the One that keeps me, that sustains me, comfort and controls me, my hiding place, my fulfillment. I have a need greater than the need for a man, greater than the need for a woman, greater than sex . . . and it's intimacy with You, Father. I can't afford to be without You. I can't live without You." This is true, real worship! And true worship is our highest purpose.

Every single person reading this book, every single person that has set foot on this earth was born with a purpose. This is why satan has tried to keep you in bondage to sexual sin: to kill your purpose. That lying murderer wants to kill your destiny. But he can't do it. God predetermined, predestined, and prearranged you and your purpose before sexual sin. For whatever reason, be it sin or the devil, your inability to recognize or carry out your purpose has not canceled your purpose. You know how I know this?

Recorded in the book of Matthew is the lineage of Jesus. Tamar who connived her way into getting pregnant by her father-in-law; Rahab, a prostitute who was used in God's plan to protect His people; David, an adulterous man who became the greatest king and a man after God's own heart; Bathsheba, who committed adultery with David, birthed the wisest King in the Bible, Solomon . . . all sinners who still lived out God's purpose in their lives. Sexual sin still does not have more power than purpose!

What God intended for your life still awaits you. Your responsibility is to recognize and identify why God created you, and then fulfill and answer that call. The only way you can do that is to get it from the One who supplied and appointed you with it. Until you do, you will continue to run an endless search for a thrill that you can only find in doing God's will. You can no longer make excuses as to why you are not fulfilling your purpose, or why you allow illegal relationships, sin or procrastination to prevent you from doing God's will. The Message translation in Proverbs 18:9 says that procrastination is equal to vandalism. Vandalism is a willful act of violating and damaging property. You are willfully killing your purpose when you procrastinate. It's just as deadly as sleeping around. So, no more vandalizing! Let's get started. Below, you will find a list of the four R's concerning your purpose and how you can fulfill it.

1. **Recognition**

The first thing you need to do is find out what your purpose is by seeking God's face. You don't have to create purpose; it already exists. God created your purpose before He made you. When He made you, He designed you specifically for it. You are already equipped and qualified for it. You just have to recognize what it is. Hints: You can naturally do it. You love to do it, and nobody can do it better than you, and you'd do it even if you couldn't get paid for it.

2. **Redirection**

Your passion for your purpose was transferred to other things and people. Your passion was in all the wrong places. Now, you have to redirect your passion and use it for your purpose. You should make every day a step toward fulfilling your purpose. This means you'll need a P.O.A—a plan of action. Without a plan, you automatically plan to fail.

A waiter or waitress always carries a pen. Make sure you have a pen and paper with you when you spend time with God. Have them also at your bedside. God will speak to you about your purpose during your private time with Him. And be prepared, there will be nights when He'll wake you up and talk to you. Habakkuk 2:2 says write it down. Then make steps toward daily, monthly, and yearly goals as He continues to reveal His will to you.

3. Responsibility

When you meet God, He's going to ask, "What did you do with what I gave you?" You are accountable to the purpose that He has given you. There are thousands, perhaps millions, of people who are suffering or are lacking something when you do not respond to your assignment. Your purpose is absolutely necessary and essential; God would have never birthed you if it wasn't.

Dr. Myles Munroe always says that the richest place in the world is the graveyard. There are millions of gifts and talents, books, inventions, lecturers, lawyers, doctors, singers, actors, and ministers who have never responded to their purpose in life. Don't go to Heaven with it, it's useless there; we need what you have here! Take the order and then go and fulfill the request.

4. Radar

You have a God-given right to protect your purpose. Use your Holy Ghost radar to screen the people who come into your life. God has your destiny predetermined. When a person comes into your life, they are either there to promote and help your purpose or they are there to destroy and kill it. There are no in-betweens. Remember, when satan wants to destroy you, he'll send a person to your life to do just that.

Have your Holy Ghost radar on when people enter into your life. The Holy Spirit will reveal the intent and motives of any destiny killers. If the radar goes off and beeps, they cannot enter. They will only blur or distort your vision! You must only cultivate relationships that are stamped and approved by God. Understand, that purpose will dictate the choices you make, the people you allow to enter your life, what's important and who is unnecessary . . . because purpose only thrives or produces in its proper environment. Get in the presence of God daily and allow him to birth your purpose. Wait on Him; walk up to Him every day and say, "Daddy, may I take your order?" Destiny is inevitable!

    I have a friend named Thelma, who has a powerful testimony. Thelma walked the streets for years as a prostitute, selling the possessions of her body. The detestable sins that she committed while walking the streets began to catch up with her. Close encounters with death, guns to her head, knives to her throat and half her body hanging out of a window (close to being thrown out of a tall building) caused her to come to her senses. It got to the point where she had to get out of it. One problem was that the pimp she worked for was not going for it. He told her, "You can't leave me after all this time. You <u>belong</u> to me."

    The night Thelma tried to leave, he kidnapped her at gunpoint and promised to kill her if she tried any attempts at getting away. "This time I won't miss," he threatened. Thelma knew that he was serious, especially after all the other times he had tried to kill her and the fact that the other victims did not survive. While he was driving on the highway and Thelma was handcuffed to the car door, Thelma started praying, "Lord, if you get me out of this one, I promise, I'll live for you." Thinking of a getaway plan, Thelma said to her kidnapping pimp, "I'm really hungry, can we stop and get something to eat?" Pulling over to a restaurant, he looked at Thelma with death in his eyes, "Thelma, we're going to go in here and get something to eat, but I swear to you that if you try anything, I will blow your brains out, right in this restaurant."

After filling themselves with food and drink, Thelma had to relieve herself and asked to be excused so she could use the restroom. *Get-away time*, she thought, until she got in the restroom and saw that there were no windows in it. She began to plead with God, "*Lord, what am I going to do? I promise you I'll live my life for you. I don't want to die. Please, get me out of this.*" Before she could finish her plea, she looked down at the toilet paper in the stall she sat in and began to write a letter on it, "If you find this letter, I am in the restaurant and I am with my former pimp. I don't want to be a prostitute anymore and he's kidnapped me. He has a gun and is trying to kill me. We are in a brown Cadillac, license plate WXY 346. PLEASE HELP."

Thelma went back to their table and the pimp said, "It's time to go." As they walked to the car, loud sirens came out of nowhere. Thelma said that you would have thought somebody tried to kill the President, "You should have seen it, Ty. It was the FBI, the CIA, DEA, the navy, the marines." Guns came out from everywhere into the face of Mr. Pimp. "You are under arrest, don't move!" Thelma was so shocked; she didn't know what was going on. She just started backing away from the car right into the arms of a plain-clothed police officer, "I'm an undercover agent, I found your letter in the bathroom," she said. Thelma fell into the arms of that woman and just wept. Talk about the power, grace and mercy of God! Don't tell me what God can't do! God will use a piece of toilet paper to save you . . . anything to save you!

The pimp is doing time in prison and Thelma's doing time on the streets, as a missionary, witnessing to people about the saving power of Jesus Christ! Every time I talk to Thelma, I ask her what she's doing and she'll respond, "Girl, I'm getting ready to go on a date. I'm about to go and get on my knees. When I was out on the streets, I was accustomed to getting down on my knees for a man. Now, no more. I get on my knees with Jesus and only for Jesus!" Talk about worshipping Him in spirit and in truth—that's real worship.

This is where your relationship with Daddy should be, where you completely let Him in and take control of your life, where the worship is sincere and genuine . . . No more secrets, no more not showing up when He calls. It's time to get rid of worldly mentality and get to real worship. You were quick to get naked and lay with someone who contaminated you, but you will cover up with God. Now, it's time to uncover, get naked, raw and real with God and allow the relationship to go from the altar to the Throne Room . . . But it's going to cost you. Oh, yes, it will. You're going to have to maintain purity. You can't be slippin' and dippin'. You are going to have to make a date with God every day and you will not be able to stand Him up. Your relationship with God is the most important aspect of your life; not even your purpose can get in the way of your time with God.

"Pray that you will not be overcome by temptation." Luke 22:40 (NLT)

I am convinced that single Christians have active sex lives because they do not have a relationship with God. Prayer is simply a relationship with Him. This is how we fall prey to temptation: lack of prayer. When I was writing the book, it had me so busy that I would attempt to give God a "five-minute" prayer. It didn't mean anything that I was doing it for Him; I still couldn't put this book before Him. One day, I tried to give Him my "five-minute prayer" and He stopped me. "Where are you going? **If you don't lay in my presence, you'll be laying in someone else's. You are not the one who's keeping you.**" It doesn't mean anything that you are delivered and free from sexual sin, you'll still need Him. You are kept by the power of the Holy Spirit. You'll need Him to maintain, you'll need Him to survive . . . You'll need Him to live. Daily intimacy is a *must*!

This is another reason why you do not see people moving to another level in God: in church for years, but no evidence of it. They'd rather stay in that category where they live only one percent of their lives for Him, never consummating the marriage they've entered in. They stay in the careful, coward zone, never committing. But you are only cheating yourself because the rewards and blessings of God outweigh the small costs.

Yes, it's a small cost in comparison to the abundance of the fulfillment you experience with God. The stagnant, spiritual droughts you find yourself in are due to the fact that you have chosen to be a comfortable Christian. That comfort level is only soothing your flesh, because on the inside, you are dying, because life outside of Christ is simply . . . death! You're either growing and living or on the decline and dying—there's no in-between.

You have to move beyond the corridors of comfort and into the center of ecstasy with Jesus. Until consummation, you'll never reach fulfillment trying to play hard-to-get with God. It's only in the complete surrendering of yourself that you reach the highest and most intense peak of your relationship with God. You'll come to find that there's always another level of intensity. This puts an end to spiritual adultery; this means no longer having a mistress or being one. Everything you've substituted God for has to go.

> "God showed how much he loves us by sending his only Son into the world so that we might have eternal life through Him. This is real love. It is not that we loved God, but that He loved us and sent His Son as a sacrifice to take away our sins . . . We know how much God loves us, and we have put our trust in Him. God is love, and all who live in love live in God, and God lives in them." I John 4:9-10, 16 (NLT)

This is real love. You are used to imitators who've prostituted you, molested you, and raped you . . . and a lot of times we have subconsciously treated God as if He was the perpetrator. From deadbeat dads who never show up, to men and women who have come and gone. But Daddy will never leave you in the window waiting for Him to pull up, and then never show up. Jesus paid that price for you while on the cross. God had forsaken Him for the sins that we committed. Since the price of sin had been paid for, God says, "I can never leave you nor forsake you. You can trust me, you've seen how much I love you and now you'll know what it's really like to be 'in love.'"

> "God is love, and all who **live in love live in God**, and God lives in them." I John 4:16 (NLT)

Everything I am is because of Jesus. My relationship with Him is the most important part of my life. There were times when I could not depend on anyone, not even my family . . . But this Man was always there, even when I was the one at fault. When I am in doubt or in confusion, I find peace in Him. In my imperfections, this Man loves me (unconditionally). When I'm hurting, sad, or discouraged, I've learned to climb in His arms, rest on the ripples in His chest and find comfort. I can tell Him anything and He still loves me. He knows all my deepest, darkest, ugliest, hidden faults . . . and He still loves me. And I love Him.

When I think about the times I strayed away and did things that displeased and hurt His heart, I shake my head and I plead my case, "Daddy, I had to be out of my mind. It was temporary insanity." In His unconditional love for me, he responds, "Daughter, case dismissed." That's my Daddy. I can't help but love Him back. He's the Lover of My Soul and no one can take His place. What man or woman do you know who can love you like this? No one! You can't even comprehend what love is until you experience Him. It's living in God, existing in Him daily that you come to know true love because that's just who He is.

> "So, no matter what I say, what I believe, and what I do, I'm bankrupt without love. Love never gives up. Love cares more for others than for self. Love doesn't want what it doesn't have. Love doesn't strut, doesn't have a swelled head, doesn't force itself on others, isn't always 'me first, doesn't fly off the handle, doesn't keep score of the sins of others, doesn't revel when others grovel, takes

pleasure in the flowering of truth, puts up with anything, trusts God always, always looks for the best, never looks back, but keeps going to the end. Love never dies." I Corinthians 13:3-8 (The Message)

God, Who is love, even in all your faults, never gives up on you. Every time that you messed up and fell, He never gave up on you, but continued to love you in spite of your downfalls and shortcomings, because love—God—never keeps score or record of sins.

> **"I, even, I am He who blots out your transgressions for My own sake; and I will not remember your sins." Isaiah 43:25**

This doesn't make me purposely sin, but it makes me all the more want to live my life consistently for Him. It's His goodness that makes me repent; it's His love that causes me to live right and holy. No, you don't always do what's right. You make mistakes, and just flat-out mess some things up sometimes. The Bible says in Lamentations 3:23 that God's mercy is new every morning. Why would God give new mercy every single morning? **For yesterday's mess-ups.**

> "The steps of a good man are ordered by the Lord, And He delights in His way. Though he falls, he shall not be utterly cast down; For the Lord upholds him with His hand." Psalms 37:23-24

This Scripture tells me that a good man or woman can love God and still screw up some things. But Daddy is always with you. There's no way you can fall and be upheld at the same time except through and by God's hand. The key is never letting go of His hand. I remember when I would go and sleep with a guy, I would feel so bad (afterwards). I would be ashamed and would try my best to stay away from God, as if He didn't see me do it. I wouldn't talk about it and every time God would try to bring it up, I would ignore Him. And Satan with his evil, foul self would taunt me, after leering me into doing it. He said, "See, look at you . . . messed up again. You'll never be right. God doesn't want to hear from you. You're going to hell. You might as well go ahead and do it again." I fell for that so many times. I didn't know any better; I had no idea about the mercy of God. I would go for weeks, sometimes months, without praying, repenting, or saying anything to God.

I remember a time when I had gone over to this other man's house and had sex with him. I was really mad at myself that time. I had been consistent in my commitment with God, had developed a relationship with Him, and had not slept with a man in years. Only to let one night of stupidity not only rob me of my purity, but rob me of God's trust and His Heart. I cried hysterically. Then, I remember hearing the sound of Daddy's voice, "Come here." Instead of running, this time, I fell right into His arms. I had experienced the true essence of 1 John 1:9, "If we confess our sins, he is faithful and just to forgive us our sins, and to cleanse us from all unrighteousness." This Scripture is for believers, sons and daughters of God. So, this means that we are subject to error, but there's a difference between "mess-ups" and practiced sin. The children of God do not make a practice or habit out of sinning. In your daily walk with God, you'll find that you may not do all the right things, but it's your relationship with God through Jesus that allows you to come before Him and say, "Daddy, I messed up. Forgive me. I want to be right with you." It's your daily relationship with the Father that prevents the mess-ups. It's in His faithfulness, His unconditional love, that He restores you and puts you in right standing with Him. **Because love never keeps a record of when it has been wronged. It's because of His love that you will find yourself having to pray 1 John 1:9 less and less.**

He never brings it back up to you because love never looks back, but always looks for the best. God sees you as His best, because you are His best. He sees Himself when he looks at you. He sees holiness, not your mistakes. God is not like man. "I'll give you one more chance." No, God does not say this, because He didn't keep a record of the last wrong you've done, your past sins.

The NLT translation in verse seven says that love never gives up, never loses faith, is always hopeful and endures through every circumstance. I don't care how many challenges you face as a single person, God never gives up on you because He knows the power of His love—it's life-changing! It'll bring you through any temptation, enticement or trap that the devil thinks he has set up for you. His love will cause you to endure, which means you'll be able to sustain and bear with patience, without yielding, to any of those temptations until God sends you the man or woman that He is calling for you to be in covenant with. The Bible tells it this way in Galatians 2:19-21 (The Message):

> "What actually took place is this: I tried keeping rules and working my head off to please God, and it didn't work. So I quit being a "law man" so that I could be God's man. Christ's life showed me how, and enabled me to do it. I identified myself completely with him. Indeed, I have been crucified with Christ. My ego is no longer central. It is no longer important that I appear righteous before you or have your good opinion, and I am no longer driven to impress God. Christ lives in me. The life you see me living is not "mine," but it is lived by faith in the Son of God, who loved me and gave himself for me. I am not going to go back on that. Is it not clear to you that to go back to that old rule-keeping, peer-pleasing religion would be an abandonment of everything personal and free in my relationship with God? I refuse to do that, to repudiate God's grace. If a living relationship with God could come by rule keeping, then Christ died unnecessarily."

It is not rules that keep a single man or woman. Neither is it self-righteousness or reliance upon your own power and ability . . . **But it is the love of God through Jesus and the relationship you have with Him that keeps you.** There are no formulas or new tricks, regulations or principles; it's through the life and example of Jesus Christ. Not through the impression that I'm saved, that I have the title Christian, but because I am one. I don't try to impress or fool God into thinking that I'm His because I attend church, sing in the choir, or quote a few Scriptures. But I imitate exactly that—the life of one who proclaims and live it as Jesus did. And this is the model:

1. Keeping My Father's Commandment (John 8:55)
2. A Lifestyle of Prayer (Matthew 26:36)
3. I'm Committed to Him (John 17:19)
4. I Honor God with My Body and Die to Self (Luke 22:42)
5. I Live by His Power and It Keeps Me (John 6:57, NLT)
6. Finish My Assignment and Live Out My Purpose (John 17:19)
7. I Am Who I Am, because of God (John 5:19)
8. I Do Nothing without Consulting Him (John 5:30)
9. I Love Him with All of Me (Mark 12:29, 30)
10. He is My Lord and My only Lover (Luke 4:8)

There's no rule keeping or religion about it . . . It's your life, one hundred percent. Because no matter what you say, what you believe, and what you do, you are bankrupt without God. It is in Him that you are saved, it is Him who delivers you, it is Him who makes and keeps you holy. It is your relationship that causes you to go from the altar into daily intimacy with Him. It is only through and because of Him, the lover of your soul, that you are single, saved, and NOT having sex! And it is only in Him that you maintain your deliverance!

"Now unto Him Who is able to keep you without stumbling or slipping or falling, and to present [you] unblemished (blameless and faultless) before the presence of His glory in triumphant joy and exultation [with unspeakable, ecstatic delight]- To the one only God, our Savior through Jesus Christ our Lord, be glory (splendor), majesty, might, and dominion, and power and authority, before all time and now and forever (unto all the ages of eternity). Amen (so be it)." Jude 24, 25 (Amplified)

Made in the USA
Monee, IL
28 June 2023

37903945R10095